System Accidents

System Accidents

Why Americans Are Injured At Work And What Can Be Done To Stop It

How to improve systems through the lens of Profound Knowledge

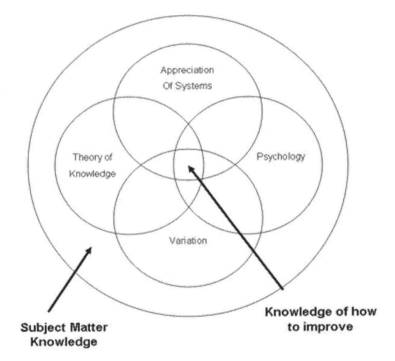

Thomas A. Smith

2009

System Accidents

If you are wondering why your safety performance has hit a plateau, read this book! Traditional safety management can only drive your safety performance so far. Until you look at the variability in the system, you will not be able to break through that plateau and deliver world-class safety performance. The time-tested techniques described in this book will provide you with the insights you'll need to a fully engage the workforce on a focused effort of designing safety into the process. Reacting to each and every accident won't get you there. Once you get the workforce started, it will take on a life of its own and become part of the organization's culture. Take safety into the 21st century...it's long overdue.

Glen Macri, Pfizer Global Operations

System Accidents will set you up to succeed. If you want to improve your safety system while respecting and elevating other systems in your organization, this book is for you. System Accidents will guide you through the development of solutions to problems and allows you to implement them thoughtfully and in a non-threatening manner. Tom's book has set the stage to remove barriers and create a win-win situations for the entire organization!

Richard Caldwell, EHS Manager, Metallurg Vanadium

When it comes to workplace safety there are two schools of thought; the traditional approach, which ultimately blames accidents on the workers, or the quality approach, which attributes accidents to the system. Tom Smith's book puts into context why his CRISP process should replace the traditional approach.

Bernard A. Sznaider CSHM, MI-OSHA Consultant(retired).

This is the closest you'll ever be to a practical understanding of the way things work, why things go wrong, and how to make things better. And it is the closest we've ever come to improving the long-term competitive position of American business.

System Accidents provides us with our best opportunity yet to solve the increasingly insoluble...how to continually renew and improve quality and productivity without compromising employee safety and long-term competitive position. But this book is not just about quality, productivity or safety. Nor is it just for the American worker. This is a book about applied leadership in behavioral and systems theory. It is a must read for all supervisors, managers, and executives in manufacturing and service industries. This is outside the box thinking about safety.

Richard S. Dillard, PMP, Performance Improvement Consultant

When it comes to safety...Tom Smith has written the call to look beyond the tired safety theory and practices of Taylor and Heinrich used in the last fifty years and use Dr Deming's principles, successfully modified for continual improvement of safety management. This is a "must read" book for any EHS professional who wants to improve EHS performance and lead the transformation to these principles of safety in an organization. These principles can integrate with the Quality and Environmental aspects of any operation to build a coherent quality, environmentally sustainable as well as a safety culture. He provides a contrast in the day of a "traditional" safety manager versus a manager with "profound knowledge" and the principles to give a glimpse of how his vision can be organized. The issue is EHS leadership to effect EHS culture change and senior management encouragement. From Machiavelli to George Bernard Shaw, we are shown that transformations are difficult...no "instant pudding"...yet Tom shows where the path begins for continual improvement of safety management.

James C Johnston, PE, CSP, CPEA
Director , Safety & Industrial Health, Wyeth

System Accidents provides a refreshing approach to critically evaluating what causes accidents that leads to human suffering and harm. As W. Edwards Deming outlined in Out of the Crisis, American companies require nothing less than a transformation of management style with industry. Tom Smith has expanded upon several key concepts and principles in Out of the Crisis and correlates to safety masterfully. System Accidents also provides a roadmap to safety culture transformation by utilizing systems thinking, statistical control, and creative problem solving as the foundation for continuous improvement in the journey to safety excellence.

Darryl C. Hill, CSP
Safety & Health Officer, ABB Inc.
Adjunct Instructor, Oakland University

Table of Contents

This book is dedicated to my wife, Shelley, who has listened to me talk about Dr. Deming, safety and management for the last 25 years.
And to all the working men and women who face hazards at work everyday.

Preface

"No amount of care or skill in workmanship can overcome fundamental faults in the system."
W. Edwards Deming

The aim of this book is to help transform how we manage safety. To transform something requires changing it. No one has been able to make changing any management system easy. This book isn't about easy. It's about putting pride, joy and fun back into safety management.

When it comes to managing safety there are basically two alternatives. One is to "meet specifications." This approach has its roots in the engineering concept of variation. As long as you meet specifications that is "good enough." The other is to make sure safety is delivered as consistently as possible. These two management philosophies, compliance with specifications vs. continual process improvement, have nothing in common with each other. They cannot be reconciled. You must choose one or the other when it comes to managing.

The former is about command and control and almost always ends up focusing on controlling what workers do. The later is concerned with controlling processes in a system to make the system do what you want so you can satisfy your customers. It doesn't take too much of a guess to know which one will be more successful.

Managing to meet specifications will get you something. It will never deliver continual improvement. When I first started working as a manager I wasn't even aware the two options existed. (Many managers today are still unaware of them.)

In 1980 I, as well as a few million other people in the US, watched an NBC White Paper, "If Japan Can...Why Can't We." At the time I was working for an insurance company as the manager of the loss control (safety) department. We used to jokingly say the insurance industry was 200 years of business unaffected by progress. For me seeing that documentary was a defining moment.

The late Dr. W. Edwards Deming, who was only shown on the last fifteen minutes of the program, delivered a simple yet profound message. He talked about quality and the fact you don't get ahead by building parts, inspecting them, removing the bad ones and sending the good ones to your customer. (How's that for keeping it simple.) You get ahead by building good parts in the first place. His message was simple and made sense yet no company I knew of at the time was doing it.

I was working with a lot of suppliers to GM, Ford and Chrysler. All of them were managing their business exactly opposite of what Deming was preaching. They built parts, performed final inspections, separated bad ones from the good (which they considered to be good quality control), scrapped or reworked the bad ones and delivered the good ones. Frankly, until I heard what Deming had to say about quality I didn't think there was much you could do about defects. As long as you gave your customers good parts that was "good enough." There was no need to worry about it since a relatively small number of bad parts got through to the customers and they really didn't complain about it. It was just a fact-of-life in mass production.

Besides, I knew these companies didn't have a clue about how to fix their quality problems and they weren't worried about it. If they didn't catch the bad parts in final inspection they would just retrieve them from their customers, replace them with good ones and that was it. Until I heard Dr. Deming I didn't think about it or realize that ultimately the customer was paying for all the bad parts. The cost was just built into the price. He said this way of running a business was foolish, would not work and it would destroy business in the long run. The suburbs of Detroit are filled with empty industrial buildings previously occupied by companies who did not heed his advice. GM, Ford and Chrysler are tragic examples of businesses destroyed by their lack of commitment to continual improvement. (Ford got it for a while Don Peterson ran it in the late 80's and early 90's and then lost its way and is fighting for its life today.)

Deming advocated many things which seemed irrational to managers at the time, like limiting the number of suppliers to reduce the variation of parts. He said it is hard enough to control variation with just one supplier let alone two, three or more. It was common practice of purchasing managers to have two or more suppliers to play them against each other to "keep them honest" or just in case one of them had to shut down production due to a fire or a strike. He pointed out if you have two suppliers you will eventually have two fires. I met many managers in the 70's and 80's who thought he was crazy.

One of his most interesting and compelling "crazy" ideas concerned the origin of most of the defects and accidents in any production or service system. He said they were mostly built into the system and not the result of workers doing things wrong. How you design and manage your systems determines how many problems, defects and employee accidents will occur. This idea struck a chord with me but over the years I've found people who are not systems thinkers don't buy it. Deep down inside they honestly believe when something goes wrong the job of management is to find out who caused it and make the guilty party pay.

I worked at a truck assembly plant my first summer after high school. My job was installing instrument panels. The job didn't require much skill and it wasn't hard physically. I paid little attention to quality because my supervisor really wasn't worried about it. As long as I made my daily quota of parts I was OK. I received minimal training of how to do the work. I don't recall ever being told to worry about quality or safety on the job.

In the 1960's and 70's dealerships were considered the last stop of the assembly line. They took care of any quality problems noticed by the customer. The philosophy was build it, ship it, sell it. In those days the general public believed most quality problems were a result of the bad work habits of people on the line. They believed vehicles built on a Fridays had the worst quality because hourly employees were either absent or drinking on their lunch hour.

I would say the quality of the vehicles was pretty much the same on a Friday as any other day. The workers themselves had little or nothing to do with it. The fact is the quality of vehicles was up to management. They designed the work system and the workers did what they were told to do. I left the job at the end of summer to go to college. I never worried about quality on the assembly line again until I listened to Deming's comments in 1980. As soon as I heard them, I knew he was a person who understood quality and work systems. The people I worked for back in 1966 did not.

I read everything I could about Dr. Deming and his philosophy. He ended up working with many American car companies, especially Ford and GM. I've met and worked with many of managers who attended his four day seminar and also worked directly with him. They responded to what he was teaching in one of three ways:

- They understood it and tried hard to practice it.
- They vaguely understood it but they weren't interested in practicing it because it was too hard to do.
- They didn't get it and could care less about his ideas. They were confident to the point of arrogance that what they were doing was the best way to manage.

Deming saw production and service as a system with inputs, processes and outputs. The outputs were a result of how management designed and ran the system. The diagram below is how he drew it for the Japanese in 1950.

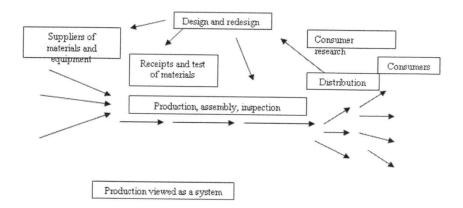

Dr. Deming's view of a system

It's a simple diagram – of a very complex system. It made me realize that if scrap and defects are the result of the system then so are employee accidents. It was my first exposure to systems thinking. It gave me a new perspective of what causes employee accidents. Ultimately it took me to a higher level of understanding what causes employee accidents and how to manage to prevent them.

Accidents are to safety what defects are to quality, outcomes of the system. Deming says most accidents (85-99%) are created by faults in the system which is designed, built and controlled by management, not the workers. (He wasn't trying to relieve the workers of their duty to work safely. He was just trying to explain how the system works.) Therefore, management is ultimately responsible for most of the outcomes of quality, productivity and safety. When it comes to safety, workers are directly affected by how management designs and runs the system, not the other way around. This idea has been difficult and even impossible for managers to accept.

Perhaps it is difficult because it is exactly the opposite of what the safety profession has taught us for the last 100 years. According to their theory, 85-88% or more of employee injuries are the direct result of the "unsafe actions" of individual workers. Consequently when it comes to safety we focus on fixing their behaviors. Most managers still believe the major cause of employee accidents is their own carelessness.

Deming's philosophy about business is to always focus on your customers. Since they ultimately define quality you must constantly work on getting the Voice of the Customer into the Voice of the Process. And then he would confuse you by explaining that customers don't know what they want. That's the tricky part. They only know what you give them. It is up to the supplier to have a close relationship with customers to find out their needs. Needs are problems for which there is no known solution.

It is up to suppliers to learn about customer needs and create products or services to satisfy them. To do this a supplier must have a dialogue with customers where both sides involved in the conversation learn something about each other. That means suppliers must listen closely to customers and come up with innovative products to satisfy their problems which create needs. (Who asked for an I-Pod?)

It struck me the customer principle was not being applied to safety management but it should be. A customer is defined as anyone who benefits from your product or service. In my mind, employees are **the customers** of safety management since they benefit the most from it. When it comes to safety on-the-job employees have expectations and needs and it is up to management to find out what they are and then take care of them. This approach will require what is called a paradigm shift.

Joel Barker, an expert on paradigms, says there are three choices you have during a paradigm shift. They are, in order of ascending impact: [1]
Keep your paradigm; change your customer.
Change your paradigm: keep your customer.
Change your paradigm: change your customer.

Each one has different challenges and results. This book is about the third choice. We have to change our safety paradigm since the one we have been using doesn't solve the problems we face in the new economy. The shift to lean management in the 21st century (Another paradigm shift.) means hourly workers will perform as much knowledge work as they do manual labor. Until now, safety has been focused on pleasing the wrong customers, the regulators. We have to change that. In the new safety paradigm management has to acknowledge that employees are the most important customers of safety, not management or regulators as was the case in the past. For that reason alone it is time for a new safety paradigm.

When you apply the customer principle to safety everything changes. The first thing you learn is there a chain of reciprocal links between customers and suppliers, i.e. management and workers. Safety management is linked to each and every worker and every one of them is a customer. Each worker is simultaneously both a customer and a supplier to their company. Consequently when management delivers a high level of safety to workers they become better suppliers of mental and manual labor to the company.

In the 1980's due to a chain of unusual circumstances I was able to apply Deming's theories about safety to the workplace. (My boss at the time was fired and not replaced for two years. It was like being in a reverse Dilbert cartoon.) Although I was a novice and didn't have the benefit of someone to guide me, it was obvious his philosophy of management worked as well for safety as it did for quality. It was certainly much better than the traditional approach I had been using.

To get managers to change their focus of safety to the needs of the individual employee will require a total transformation. The overarching goal of traditional safety management is to maintain the status quo by meeting specifications. People don't realize when you manage to meet specifications you will never achieve continual improvement. It's because once you have met specifications, safety or otherwise, all kinds of variation still exist. Some managers try to combine the two approaches, meeting specifications in some areas and striving for continual improvement in others. But the methods and techniques contradict each other. Instead of creating synergy the combination of the two methods cancel each other out and make matters worse.

An example is the matter of trust. Trusting people is an either or proposition. You either trust employees or you don't. As you will see the management system designed by Frederick Taylor prevents trust between management and workers. A positive, constructive and effective management culture comprises of managers who trust workers will do a good job and their actions reflect this. Mutual trust is absolutely necessary for the modern methods of lean management to work. In this environment employees are given much more responsibility and authority to act and make decisions on their own. Managers must put their trust in workers or this system will not work. A company cannot afford to pay employees to perform the non-value added work of monitoring other employees to ensure they are doing what is expected of them. It is just too inefficient and expensive.

Most traditional safety management activities include safety inspections, audits, accident investigations, incentive programs and motivational schemes. These activities exist to control and monitor workers behaviors. The unspoken but understood rationale behind them is they are necessary because employees can't be trusted to work safely on their own. Management believes employees need to be watched, coached and motivated to work safely. I know of one company where management talked about the need for trust to exist between them and hourly workers yet they required every employee be subjected to a search of their lunch box as they exited the plant. Talk about a mixed message!

Traditional safety management creates a parent/child relationship between managers and workers. Management treats workers like children but holds them accountable to standards reserved for adults. I've seen many managers place the responsibility for an accident directly on the injured worker and counsel them that "even a child would know better." Which begs the question, is the problem because the safety of the job is more complex than the manager understands it to be; or is it because the employee doesn't have the ability to grasp how to work safely? In either case the problem seems to be more about management than the individual worker.

All theories are correct – in some world. If you believe people would not get hurt if only they would do things right the first time you would be right. Unfortunately this theory only goes so far. It won't solve any problems in even the most simple work system. That is where systems thinking, a new way of looking at the world of work comes into play. Systems thinking has been described as the discipline of seeing wholes. It helps us realize unsafe acts and unsafe conditions are actually symptoms not causes of a problem.

Most managers will tell you they believe people do not come to work with the hidden agenda to make scrap or injure themselves. But that's as far as it goes. The fact is, once production starts their actions contradict their words. It's obvious traditional safety management provides an inadequate explanation of why accidents occur at work. To find the answer requires a new way of thinking about things. Deming called this new way of looking at the world profound knowledge.

Profound knowledge involves basic understanding of four things; systems, variation, psychology and how we obtain knowledge. To learn and apply it does not require a PhD. as the label would seem to imply. A basic understanding of the four elements and how they fit together is enough to put it to good use. For example; learning and applying profound knowledge will help you;

1. Change your fundamental thinking about safety.
2. Identify what's important about safety.
3. Understand and solve safety problems with a new point of view and new methods.
4. Provide leadership to sustain this new way of managing safety.

I've met many people who claim they've adopted Deming's theory of quality for safety only to be disappointed when I see how they actually run their operations. It's as though they've learned the words to a song but they can't carry the tune. It's hard for managers to apply his theories because they are the opposite of what's been taught and practiced for so long. For example, there has been an almost universal failure of American manufacturers to master and achieve lean manufacturing, which is inherent in his philosophy of quality. They have learned the vocabulary with words like pull, flow, just in time and takt time. They can even tell you what they mean. But when it comes to doing it they just can't make the transformation away from command and control batch and queue methods.

Toyota, considered one of the best at lean production, studied Dr. Deming's philosophy in the 1950's and you can see his influence in their methods even today. Their leaders who worked with him gained a deep understanding of what he said and used it to improve their approach to managing. They continue to build on it. In the 1980's and 90's American managers also studied Dr. Deming. They tried to copy or mimic what other companies did with his ideas. That didn't work so they discarded or ignored Deming in search of other silver bullets or instant pudding. The results have been mostly disappointing. A lot of those companies have disappeared or are now in bankruptcy proceedings.

One reason for the lack of success is the way American managers think about business and run their operations. Most American managers determine the price of their products using the basic cost principle:

$$Costs + Profit = Selling\ Price$$

Using this approach all costs are paid for by the consumer. The producer has no reason to worry about total costs or waste. If the price of materials increases they are just passed along to the consumer.

Companies that are truly into continual improvement and lean production use a non-cost principle:

$$Selling\ Price - Costs = Profit$$

In this world, competitors and the market drives the selling price. Profit is what remains after subtracting the costs from the selling price.

A sure fire way to increase profit is to reduce waste. When a company is totally committed to cost reduction as the way to increase profits it will be motivated to reduce waste every day. It exists to satisfy the customer. In this world employee accidents are the worst form of waste! Since you don't have any extra employees on your payroll if one of them gets injured you have a real serious problem. A business that is managed to reduce costs uses systems thinking and lean methods which are almost exactly opposite of the rules and methods of mass production. It is a different way of thinking with new rules, new methods and new ways of solving problems.

A few years ago I was working with a supervisor skilled in mass production. I learned he had reduced the cost of a part by eliminating one person in a two person operation. Unfortunately, the operation resulted in numerous back injuries costing thousands of dollars in workers compensation and the need to train new employees to replace the people who were injured. I asked him if he would consider restoring the second employee and he said absolutely not. He explained his boss was very pleased with the increase in profit of the single person operation and he would be punished for the increased costs.

Then I asked how the costs of the employee injuries and turnover were being accounted for. He said he didn't know and didn't care. All he knew was they weren't in his job costs so it didn't matter to him. He did not have the mindset to reduce costs. He succeeded in reducing the hard costs but paid no attention to total costs. Those costs were off into the Milky Way. They were not for him to worry about. He couldn't see them but they were somewhere. At some point the plant would have to pay for them. They just didn't have to account for them. If they showed up later in the form of an increase in workers compensation insurance they would just be added to the costs and passed on to the customer. They become part of the hidden factory management ignores every day. That plant is now out of business.

I can tell you in the past people could not see anything wrong with the supervisor's approach. He was getting all he could out of his operation. They would figure there's nothing he can do about it anyway so he should just keep production going. But managing the situation using the non-cost principle puts things in a different perspective so people realize they must manage differently. When you do this you have to rethink how you will manage safety as well. This example shows how lean can be mean. The workers end up paying the price for efficiency in the form of accidents. The academic studies of lean manufacturing have focused on wringing out labor costs but leave out what happens to safety of the individuals left to run the jobs.

To appreciate and understand Deming's ideas and lean manufacturing most people will have to unlearn a lot of what they currently believe to be true. Like Mark Twain said; *'It's not the things you don't know that will hurt you. It's what you know for certain that isn't so.'* That's what does the real damage.

This is not a how to book. It's more about why and a little bit of what to do. Its purpose is threefold; first to give the reader a quick history lesson of how traditional safety management evolved; second is to provide a new theory of continual improvement of safety management and third; to help the reader lead as opposed to manage the transformation to a new paradigm of safety management.

Joel Barker says when a new paradigm is adopted everything goes back to zero. After reading this book I hope you find many reasons to learn and apply a new safety paradigm. My hope is it will give you a new way of looking at what causes accidents. Then you can begin the journey of managing for **C**ontinual **R**enewal and **I**mprovement of **S**ystem/Safety **P**erformance, or what I've come to call CRISP²™. My first boss used to tell me, *"Just remember, there's always a better way!"* So let's get started and find it.

Part I

How we got here

The aim of Part I is to examine how the traditional safety model came about. First we'll examine Frederic Taylor's ideas about management and explain the ties between Taylorism (as Taylor's philosophy came to be known) and Herbert W. Heinrich's safety management theory. We'll also look at some of the major flaws and effects of their theories.

Introduction

> *"We are going to win and the industrial West is going to lose out; there's not much you can do about it because the reasons for your failure are within yourselves. Your firms are built on the Taylor model. Even worse, so are your heads. With your bosses doing the thinking while the workers wield the screwdrivers, you're convinced deep down that this is the right way to run a business. For you the essence of management is getting the ideas out of the heads of the bosses into the hands of labor. We are beyond the Taylor model."*
> Konosuke Matsushita, Founder Matsushita Electronics, 1987

This is a book about safety at work. But not in the way most people usually think about it. American managers and the public in general, have a stereotype in mind when they think of safety management. It's become a safety paradigm. In *Future Edge*, Joel Barker a futurist who helped make the word popular in management circles in the 1980's and 90's, defined paradigm. He said:

"A paradigm is a set of rules and regulations (written or unwritten) that does two things: 1.) It establishes or defines boundaries. 2.) It tells you how to behave inside the boundaries in order to be successful." (Page 32)

The traditional view of safety management held by most managers, including top management, starts with the idea that safety is just a matter of complying with and enforcing safety rules and regulations (The boundaries). This is done by conducting safety inspections, completing accident investigations and if these don't work implementing a safety incentive program. Motivating employees to work safely is deemed a necessary management activity since managers believe employees can't or won't do it on their own. (These activities control how you behave as a safety manager so you will be successful when it comes to managing safety.)

This safety paradigm is based on the fact managers believe most employee accidents are caused by the unsafe actions of the workers. Part of the reason they think this way is because they are task oriented and employ single event thinking exclusively. But mostly they think this way because that's what they have been taught.

The rules for managing safety were developed from what I call the Taylor/Heinrich management paradigm. Frederic Taylor's ideas established the command and control, single event thinking which dominates American management as Mr. Matsushita points out. Few people in the general population know it, but by the 1950's another gentleman by the name of Herbert W. Heinrich integrated his views about safety with Taylor's ideas on management and the traditional safety paradigm was born

Paradigms help us solve problems. They tell us what problems are important and then guide us on how to go about solving them. We adopt them because they do work. In the beginning they solve most of the problems in their domain. They are very useful but eventually when a paradigm can't solve all of the problems in its domain we start to work on finding a new one. American management in general has been searching and struggling to develop a new management paradigm since the 1980's. Because of people such as Deming, Juran and Drucker some progress has been made. Safety management is also struggling to adopt a new paradigm but the progress in this area has been very slow.

Some facts about the safety problem

According to US Bureau of Labor Statistics (BLS) from 1992 through 2005, 84,353 workers in the U.S. were killed on the job! These were ordinary people who left their homes and families, went to work one day and didn't return. They weren't involved in a tragedy such as the Titanic in which 1,522 lives were lost. They were just trying to do their jobs. We would have to have 55 Titanics to equal the number of lives lost at work just from 1992 – 2005!

A total of 4.3 million nonfatal injuries and illnesses were reported in private industry workplaces during 2004 alone! (One injury every 7.3 seconds.) Approximately 2.2 million injuries and illnesses were cases with days away from work. These injuries happened in spite of the fact the manufacturing sector lost more than three million jobs between 1998 and 2003! These cases occurred at a rate of 4.8 per every 100 workers.

Nonfatal workplace injuries and illnesses among private industry employers in 2006 occurred at a rate of 4.4 cases per 100 equivalent full-time workers—a decline from 4.6 cases in 2005. Similarly, the number of nonfatal occupational injuries and illnesses reported in 2006 declined to 4.1 million cases, compared to 4.2 million cases in 2005. There were an additional 5,703 fatalities in 2006!

It's estimated worker injuries cost the U.S. economy over $122 billion dollars a year. From 1975 through 2007 the budget for OSHA, the Federal watchdog for worker safety, has totaled $9,480,310,000! Private industry also spends billions on managing safety every year. There's no denying safety, or lack of it, has a huge impact on business and society. I'm not saying safety of American workers hasn't improved, from some viewpoints it has. It just hasn't improved enough.

Ironically during this same period a lot of manufacturing companies spent millions of dollars to improve quality and achieve a goal of 3.4 defects per millions of parts which theoretically delivers zero defects to customers. Businesses also shed millions of manufacturing jobs during this period and continue to shed them to this day. Makes you wonder if management thinks parts are more important than people.

Mr. Matsushita warned us about the dangers of Taylorism in 1987, but while a new management paradigm evolves American managers still practice Taylor's fundamental principles of how to manage people. We've updated the language and disguised Taylorism in many ways but it is still alive and well. For example the latest addition to management vocabulary is to refer to employees as "human capital." Some people refer to this as Neo-Taylorism. Sadly, safety management has not been able to break free of negative aspects of Taylorism.

The facts speak for themselves. Safety management needs a new paradigm. To create it we need to look at the current one.

In the beginning: Scientific Management

I would prefer to see skepticism directed at the status quo, rather than employed in its service. Alfie Kohn

According to Peter Drucker, one of the most influential and important people of management in the 20th century and beyond was Frederick W. Taylor. Taylor's paper, *The Principles of Scientific Management* written in 1911, changed forever how we look at and manage work systems. They may not be aware of it but most American managers to the current day practice Taylorism in some form or another. (Talk about making a difference!)

Frederick W. Taylor was born on March 20, 1856, in Philadelphia, Pennsylvania. He developed his theory of Scientific Management from 1880 to 1911. Taylor wanted to improve efficiencies of workers and he did so as a consultant to many companies. His approach was radical at the time and fundamentally changed how workers would do their jobs. The fact is companies throughout the world have used his methods or variations of it since he introduced it in the 1880's. However, as science and knowledge about work advanced, most of his ideas were adjusted and adapted to meet criticism directed at his system. And there was plenty.

Taylor was a pioneer in the field of time studies and functional management. He sounds like one of those guys that never met a stopwatch he didn't like. He wanted to increase worker productivity in manufacturing and at the same time to promote harmony between management and labor. Unfortunately, when his ideas were put into practice that's not how things worked out. Through empirical studies, Taylor advanced the techniques of steel manufacturing. He was an engineering consultant to various firms, including Bethlehem Steel Company. (Bethlehem ceased operations in 2004, a year short of its 100th anniversary.) He was a dominant force within the American Society of Mechanical Engineers, serving as vice president from 1904 until he was elected president in 1906. After retiring from active engineering at age forty-five, he continued to praise scientific management from his estate near Philadelphia while his critics vilified it.

Taylorism, as it has come to be known, employs a mechanistic view of the organization and the workers. He was one of the first people to think this way about work and he designed a management system to "control" what workers did and how they did it. Taylor's ideas of management dominated the twentieth century and are practiced in various forms today.

U.S. managers believe Taylor fell out of fashion long ago but a lot of what is taught and practiced by managers in business schools today is based on his ideas. In his time it was believed if you gave people any leeway they would take advantage of the company. (This is one idea today's managers certainly haven't given up.) To countermand this he devised a system to put certain types of people in charge of designing the system and others who would do the work, i.e. manual labor vs. management. Here are some of the things he said:

> ...*Hardly a competent workman can be found who does not devote considerable time to seeing just how slowly he can go and still convince his employer he is going at a good pace.*
> ...*Under our system a worker is told just what he is to do and how he is to do it. Any improvement he makes upon the orders given is fatal to his success.*
> ...*the workman who is best suited to handling pig iron is unable to understand the real science of doing this class of work. He is so stupid that the word "percentage" has no meaning to him, and he must consequently be trained by a man more intelligent than himself into the habit of working in accordance with the laws of this science before he can be successful.*

To his credit, in the later years of his life when he realized companies were focusing on the negative things of his scientific management it is said he changed his views. He regretted what was being done to working men and woman in the name of scientific management.

Taylor's four duties of managers

Taylor applied his "scientific management" principles with enthusiasm and preciseness. He was described as having a mania for efficiency. He listed the *four duties for management* in his article on scientific management and they were revolutionary at the time: [3]

First. They develop a science for each element of a man's work, which replaces the old rule-of-thumb method.

It must be remembered when Taylor started working with large companies, such as Bethlehem Steel in the 1880's, work was quite different than today. In Taylor's time workers, who were considered true craftsmen, knew more about how the actual job was performed. He believed workers kept this knowledge to themselves rather than sharing it with others and management. They did this to protect their jobs. Taylor's approach took the planning away from workers and put it in the hands of management.

Second. They scientifically select and then train, teach, and develop the workman, whereas in the past he chose his own work and trained himself as best he could. Taylor advocated a careful study of each man to determine if he could meet the physical and mental labor required to produce at the rate management determined was possible. Unfortunately this quickly led to thinking of people as bionic machines.

Third. They heartily cooperate with the men so as to ensure all of the work being done in accordance with the principles of the science which has been developed.

Taylor assumed that once his methods were enacted and productivity was improved, employees pay would be increased and the "kindly cooperation of management" would naturally unfold. This assumption never really materialized and it dismayed him later in his life.

Fourth. There is an almost equal division of the work and the responsibility between the management and the workmen. The managers take over all work for which they are better fitted than the workmen, while in the past almost all of the work and the greater part of the responsibility were thrown upon the men.

Taylor thought the mental labor of management vs. manual labor was a 50/50 proposition. In reality his approach created the "park your brains at the door" syndrome in which management does all the thinking and employees just pick up their brains when they go home at night because they aren't going to need them to do their jobs. Management has done all the thinking for the workers. Taylor did not believe people who did manual labor had the cognitive skills to learn the "new types of work done by management." Remember, things were a lot different back then.

Taylorism improved the productivity of workers and transformed craft production to mass production. His system worked wonders and variations of it have been applied and are still practiced. But because of its flaws his ideas were not appreciated by everyone (especially unions) and scientific management would eventually fade from favor in management circles. Or so it seemed.

Taylor's organization

In Taylor's day work was typically overseen by a single foreman. He replaced him with eight different men who he said would be "expert teachers" of the workers. Their duties were: planning department, an inspector, gang boss, speed boss, repair boss, route clerk and disciplinarian. Each of these men were chosen for their own knowledge and skill and they could all show the worker exactly how they were supposed to do the job they were assigned.

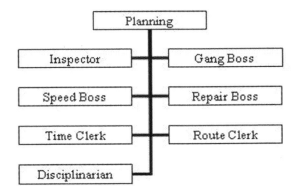

Taylor's organization chart

This is the organization chart of Taylor's Scientific Management. You can see the start of bureaucracy and the separation of managers from manual labor. Taylor placed all of the mental labor with management. Managers were to show the workers the best and fastest way to do their work, but not necessarily the safest. (I found it interesting that the word safety is not used anywhere in Taylor's document on Scientific Management.)

Taylor's ideas had positive and negative impact on managing a business. They definitely improved productivity but there was a huge backlash against him. There's no denying his approach changed forever the ideas about how work was to be done. In his time people who did manual labor were looked upon as having a noble skill. But his system broke work down to a mere series of repetitive motions. Although American managers maintain they are no longer used, much of what is being taught and practiced today is based on many of Taylor's principles. The renowned management expert Peter Drucker believed every productivity improvement effort in the last hundred years, including Japanese, is based on principles Taylor created.

Brian Joiner, a well-known quality guru said of Taylor's scientific management, "The Japanese threw out the bureaucracy and the 'white-collar think, blue-collar do,' and we kept those two pieces and threw out the part about scientific analysis of work. They kept the good part and threw out the chaff, we did the reverse."[4] Unfortunately, Joiner's assessment is quite accurate.

Flaws of Scientific Management

Below are some of the flaws of scientific management and a brief commentary of how they are still used by managers today – Neo-Taylorism.[5]

1. The belief that management control is the way to improve productivity. Taylor's idea of removing the knowledge the workers had as craftsmen and putting it with management hasn't changed to this day. He believed in strict compliance with standards set by management for the workers to follow. He called for "enforced cooperation" to make this happen. (Evidently, he didn't know what an oxymoron was.)

   Neo-Taylorism applied today. Managers practice this today by doing things like creating a culture in which the boss is the customer. Even worse is management answering to the stock market analyst instead of the customers who buy its products and services. They also rely on manipulating the workforce by through the constant application of rewards and punishments.

   Safety management has focused almost exclusively on the behavior of workers as the way to control the frequency of accidents. As if everything else in the system is working correctly. This has created the dependence on *behaviorism* and positive reinforcement as the key tool for improving safety.

Contrast this with the new management tools of continual improvement which seeks to gain control – statistical control of the system, not control of behaviors of the individual workers.

2. Managers believe it is possible for them to create the optimal process. Workers just need to do what they are told and everything will come out alright. They think they have supplied all the information and any deviation of outcomes is a result of people not doing it right the first time. All information is assumed to be knowable.

Neo-Taylorism applied today. Managers who exhort people to "do it right the first time." A manager who thinks this way either ignores or denies variation. In his world variation doesn't exist. Other people cause things to go wrong when they don't follow instructions so it's their fault when problems are created in production or service. Management induces competition within its own walls. They do this by setting up quotas and challenging departments to beat each other. This leads to all kinds of negative consequences and demoralizes the workforce. All of it being done because that's the way we did it in the past. This approach has destroyed companies and their suppliers.

Neo-Taylorism still fixates on what the workers are doing wrong. All of the recent bankruptcies of American automotive companies and their suppliers (8 of the top 50 suppliers declared bankruptcy in 2006.) have one common solution put forth by management. They believe they must reduce the cost of labor so they work hard to break the contracts they negotiated with them. Little is done about the management team and their methods that put these companies in the situation. As a matter of fact they are rewarded by having large bonus programs set up so they will stay with the sinking ship. Then they move operations off shore where labor is cheaper. All of this effort even though we know direct labor is responsible for only 10-15% of the total costs of a product.

Today American companies use "standardized work" as a method to improve productivity. The problem is they don't allow the standards, especially safety standards, to be improved. Then there is the belief that certification is a guarantee of quality. Think about all of the recalls in the auto industry and the fact that almost every company involved in them is ISO certified.

Safety management applies Taylor's approach to standards and threw out the thinking of Henry Ford who invented the production line. Ford understood that some standards are necessary such as when you are talking about weights or measures. An inch should always be an inch and a quart should always be a quart.

Standardizing a method however is different. Doing a job safely is something that should always be improved. What was the best way to do something yesterday will not necessarily be the best way to do it in the future. We can see all kinds of examples of yesterday's standards that we would not think of using today. (Using leeches to bleed patients comes to mind.) This can also be said of each employee. What is safe for one person may not be safe for another.

Ford pointed out correctly that today's standards supersede the past and tomorrow's will supersede today's. Standardization of methods should be done with the intent of always improving them.

Instead of improving safety standards, managers have also fallen prey to resorting to exhort people to put forth their best efforts to follow the safety standards as a method to ensure safety. When it comes to safety, management tries to get the most out of people by using as incentive programs and employee-of-the-month posters instead of taping their mental labor about how to make the job safer.

Many safety managers will create self-imposed competition for better safety performance. They do this by pitting one department, division or plant against the other by comparing their safety records. They call this friendly competition, an oxymoron if there ever was one. They may also link manager's incentive pay to the safety performance of their operation. This does nothing to improve safety but a lot to destroy the morale of management and employees.

Contrast this with the emphasis continual improvement puts on working harmoniously to improving the system by studying and understanding variation, systems and statistical control.

3. Management recognizes only one cause of defects: People. Since management had designed what it believes to be the "optimal" system the only thing that could go wrong was the workers messing things up.

Neo-Taylorism applied today. Today managers use posters, slogans, rewards and awards as though these are positive actions by management. They may also ask employees to sign pledges to do quality work. In my opinion, doing a small positive thing to avoid doing something really positive in a big way is actually a negative activity. The assumption here is the system designed by management is just fine. It would work perfectly if only the workers do what they've been told to do. In lieu of trinkets, employees, shareholders and customers would prefer truly excellent operations that reduce costs, accidents and improve morale.

Take the concept management has about a root cause, especially when it is applied to an accident. You can always make a case that a particular person messed up and label it as the root cause. That doesn't make it so. We now realize defects and accidents are the result of a combination of many things that work together and against each other and these are influenced more by management than the workers.

Management acts as the judge of all things. That is why Management by Objectives is still practiced in American companies. In MBO, management sets the goals for subordinates (a word I believe should now be banished from any and all management language) and they are expected to achieve them but they often do not have the means to do it.

Managers who think this way design processes and don't know how they will actually perform. They don't really care since they won't be affected like the workers who will lose their jobs or be injured if the plans fail. You will often find processes that are unsafe, designed by engineers who will never even see what they have created let alone work in the conditions.

Managers looking for ways to make things look good but never really fix the quality and safety of the process. They are always seeking a quick fix or flavor-of-the-month so production can stay at maximum levels. If they can find some instant pudding for patching problems instead of really solving them, they use it. For managers, the easiest and most obvious thing to fix when things go wrong is the worker.

Contrast this with the emphasis of continual improvement that views the work population more like a symphony orchestra. The performance of which depends on each individual unit working together not in competition with each other.

4.　　Lack of systems thinking. Taylor focused on the performance of the individual workers. He did not see or allow them to interact with any other workers or the system

Neo-Taylorism applied today. Workers are evaluated individually not collaboratively. Motivation schemes to emphasize the contribution of individual workers. Celebration of the hero or cowboy mentality to save the day when things go wrong with no thought of where they were when things were designed wrong in the first place. Policies that put departments and people in direct competition with each other. Trying to improve one part of the organization with no thought of how it impacts other parts. Saving costs in one area may wreak havoc for some other area.

Safety management applies a one size fits all mentality. The most obvious example is setting safety rules in a blanket fashion, i.e. all areas of a plant require everyone to wear safety glasses since some people have complained about having to wear them when they walk through a particular area.

Contrast this with the emphasis of continual improvement that makes management's job to remove barriers that prevent people from taking pride and joy in their jobs.

5. Viewing workers as bionic machines. Taylor set the stage for applying the psychological theories of B.F. Skinner to work. The thought processes of workers were removed from the equation of getting work done. Skinner was a man who studied animals and applied what he learned to human beings.

Neo-Taylorism applied today. Managers do not recognize what the impact of the system has on the workers. The shuffling of managers around as though they only need a limited amount of experience to understand work processes. Giving extrinsic rewards instead of developing systems that allows intrinsic motivation and joy in work. Setting numerical goals without any thought of what methods will be used to achieve them.

Safety applies this when not treating the workers as the customers of safety. Again, one size fits all when it comes to things such as personal protective equipment or ergonomics.

I've seen numerous examples of Neo-Taylorism in hundreds of plants I've worked with over the last 30 years. Work processes designed that are error inducing or certain to cause injuries to workers. For example, a plant I worked with had 40 punch presses with every two hand palm control installed so the workers had to reach above their shoulders to activate them. For those of you who aren't familiar with ergonomic design, this is one of the worst positions to have people perform repetitive motion. Every employee working in the area complained of pain to their shoulders and back.

Management's explanation for this configuration was that an OSHA inspector approved it. Evidently, two years prior to my visit an OSHA inspector accepted the location of the controls. Management interpreted this as the de jure standard and said they would be violating OSHA regulations if they changed it. Even though employees were experiencing excruciating shoulder and back pain and the most recent OSHA inspector indicated he would not oppose relocation of the controls. In reality, management did not want to spend the money to move the controls so they treated the feedback from the first inspector as though it was cast in stone. They never did change the configuration. The plant was eventually shut down.

In another example, an engineer bragged to me about the fact the company had a computer system that could signal if any of their assembly lines anywhere in the world was shut down for more than 30 seconds. I subsequently spent some time in one of those plants and saw all kinds of shut downs with no real effort by anyone to find out what went wrong but all kinds of urgency to get them up and running as fast as possible. It occurred to me the computer system was a total waste of time and money. In a high quality manufacturing system you know production does not go on without problems. You want employees to shut down the line when a bad part is made or other problems identified so you can stop it from being sent to the next operation. Since shut downs are expected there is no need to install an expensive way to monitor them.

He didn't understand the fact the system was just a bunch of unnecessary and expensive technical gimmickry. Top management used it to check on things and make it look like they knew everything that was going on at all times. They got a lot of data about production but they sure weren't going to do anything constructive with it. They had no intention of translating data into information and using it to gain knowledge. They set it up so they didn't have to interact personally with the people running things. It was the ultimate sophisticated game of gotcha.

While working in one of these plants I saw two safety backup systems fail to work concurrently, resulting in an extensive interruption of production. No one could ever tell me what caused the problem. On another day a hoist failed and a vehicle dropped violently to the floor. (No one was injured so no corrective action was taken.) Management was making everyone share responsibility so no one had to do anything about problems in the system.

On their own any one of these flaws can do some real damage. The multiplying effect of combinations of two or more of them can make things even worse. But if you look honestly at companies today it would be rare to find one not trapped in some form of Neo-Taylorism and totally unaware of the problems it causes, especially in the area of safety.

This ignorance creates one of two conditions and either can be fatal to the short and long term success of any business endeavor. They are:

- Management of the organization is in a crisis and doesn't know it.
- Management is certain of things that aren't so. (They believe Neo-Taylorism is the best way to manage.)

Both of these directly impact safety performance. Some managers seem to have an intuitive grasp of the problems with Neo-Taylorism for managing work systems, but at the same time they ignore or miss the impact it has on managing safety.

Herbert W. Heinrich, Father of Safety Management

About the time Taylor's Scientific Management was gathering momentum in the 1920's-30's Herbert W. Heinrich, considered the father of industrial safety, was working for the Travelers Insurance Company in the Engineering and Inspection department. It was here he gathered data on industrial accidents and formulated his theories on accident causes and their prevention. He was one of the first people to apply critical thinking to safety and develop theories about what causes accidents on-the-job. He created what could be considered the first paradigm for industrial safety management. Since Taylor left safety out of his management system, Heinrich came along and filled the void. He had an open field in which to work

He tried to vigorously apply "science in accident prevention" and believed safety should be managed the same way Taylor managed production. He believed the main work of the accident-prevention engineer was related to the accident and its prevention. But he was influenced by Taylor's ideas which were task oriented and guided by single event thinking.

Heinrich believed the activities of accident prevention must focus on factors "immediately preceding the accident itself; these being the unsafe act and/or the mechanical hazard, and the proximate reasons why these exist." Heinrich's approach for managing safety parallels Taylor's view of using of individual experts to design the one best way to do a job. It's been with us in one form or another ever since. Both of them ignored Henry Ford's advice about standards which he spelled out in his 1926 book, Today and Tomorrow, and adhered to the idea that a safety standard was not something to be trifled with.

So Heinrich adds another box on Taylor's org chart below:

Heinrich's organization chart introducing safety management

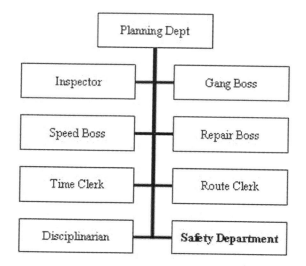

Heinrich's 10 Axioms for industrial safety- Their flaws and effects

Heinrich developed 10 axioms for industrial safety. These constituted his basic philosophy of industrial accident prevention. His axioms, their flaws compared to modern quality methods and their effect on safety management are as follows: [6]

1. *The occurrence of an injury invariably results from a completed sequence of factors – the last one of these being the accident itself. The accident in turn is invariably caused or permitted by the unsafe act of a person and/or a mechanical or physical hazard.*
   Flaw: Heinrich put the focus of safety management on controlling the behaviors of workers by emphasizing their unsafe acts are the major cause of accidents. "Control" in his world centers on making the worker do what management desires. This tracks with Taylor's proposal to take control away from the workers and put it in the hands of management. It also ignores or denies the interconnections between all things

the workers are exposed to in the system from the day they are hired.

Effect: For Heinrich, safety management's main focus is on trying to make workers behave safely, whatever that means.

Current safety programs do talk about systems but not in the true sense of systems thinking. Safety management uses linear thinking, evidenced in the domino effect theory Heinrich used to explain and understand accident causes. If you accept this idea you focus on the person or a single event and not the entire system. You also believe that if you can remove any single event in the linear progression the accident will not occur. It is the beginning of the root cause mentality as a method for preventing accidents.

2. *The unsafe acts of persons are responsible for the majority of accidents.*
Flaw: This has been the legacy and myth of Heinrich. He postulated 88% of injuries are the result of "unsafe acts" of people. Unsafe acts are often the last thing you see just before an accident occurs but they are not necessarily **the cause** of the accident. It's just easier to identify them.

This is similar to the story about the drunk looking for his keys under a street light at midnight. A passerby asks him what he is doing and he replies he is looking for his lost keys. The person asks him where he thinks he lost them and the drunk replies "in the driveway." The person asks, then why aren't you looking for them in the driveway? And the drunk replies, because this is where the light is.

You can find current articles on safety management and advertisements for companies reinforcing this "fact." Heinrich borrowed the idea from Taylor who believed management could design the best way to work and if the outcome was different than what management planned it was the fault of workers for not following instructions. Since quality and safety are both outcomes of the management system it seems to be a logical conclusion. If workers would only do what they're told they wouldn't get hurt.

In fact, this is exactly the opposite of systems thinking used in modern quality methods. In this world unsafe acts and conditions are considered symptoms of poor management. Single event thinking consistently confuses symptoms for causes. Until the 1980's most American managers fixated on blaming employees for the primary cause of defective products. It wasn't until Deming and his quality theory was rediscovered in 1980, that people realized 85-99% of all defects are built into the system and not the fault of workers. Managers had to admit workers aren't the main reason for poor quality. It's the management system and processes in a system that causes the problems.

You can't deny workers do commit unsafe actions. But you have to understand their unsafe actions are much more a product of the management system and stem from things workers cannot control. This does not relieve workers from their effort to work safely. It is just recognition that most unsafe actions are not intentional on the part of workers.

Effect: Modern safety management was overtaken by the psychology theory of B.F. Skinner, whose theory of *behaviorism* fit perfectly with single event thinking. Behavior-based safety (BBS) provided a fertile ground for a Skinnerian view to be applied without thinking critically about it. As BBS took over safety management in the 1980's and 90's, less attention was paid to advancement of accident causation theory in industrial safety. Management was very content to focus on the short term solution of getting workers to behave correctly (patching the problem) instead of truly preventing safety problems.

3. *The person who suffers a disabling injury caused by an unsafe act, in the average case has had over 300 narrow escapes from serious injury as a result of committing the very same unsafe act. Likewise, persons are exposed to mechanical hazards hundreds of times before they suffer injury.*

Flaw: This perpetuates the myth that management should monitor employees to see if they can catch people performing unsafe acts and remind them to work safely before they eventually have a serious injury. It's about the same as believing that accidents are a result of fate, chance, luck, hope and magic. The logic also appears flawed since an employee could have the accident the very first time he committed an unsafe act or if he doesn't have an accident during the 300 exposures he is more susceptible to injury with each new exposure. It begs the question, if an employee is being exposed continually to some unsafe condition, what is management doing all the while it was going on to correct the situation? It also reinforces the bias to blame the worker for accidents since they are supposedly given plenty of advanced warnings before an accident occurs.

Effect: This reinforced BBS as the primary safety tool. Again, the majority of the action by management focuses on watching employees while they work to catch them and remind them, using positive reinforcement, that they are not behaving safely. This makes it convenient for management to pass on its responsibility for safety to the worker and allows them to ignore the more important tasks of studying and improving safety in the system. The approach creates barriers to using prevention and continual improvement methods for safety. Focusing on the worker to prevent accidents is equal to focusing on the worker to prevent defects.

4. *The severity of an injury is largely fortuitous – the occurrence of the accident that results in injury is largely preventable.*

Flaw: Safety management is obsessed with the idea that all accidents are preventable. I used to teach it myself until I became aware of systems thinking and applied it to safety management. Even Heinrich found that at least 2% of accidents are just not preventable but safety managers tend to ignore this fact.

Effect: Encourages victims to believe there isn't much you can do to reduce the seriousness of an accident and all accidents are preventable. It's the old adage that hindsight is 20/20 vision. After you've had an accident you can always look back and think of things you might have done to avoid it. Unfortunately, prior to the accident you may not have been able to comprehend the accident would take place.

5. *The four basic motives or reasons for the occurrence of unsafe acts provide the guide to the selection of appropriate corrective measures.*

Flaw: Heinrich attempted to explain the remedial actions to prevent unsafe acts of people. Ironically they exist because of system problems that cause workers to commit them. He never realizes, and neither did Taylor, management could and should focus its energy and resources on improving the work systems to reduce product defects and employee accidents in the first place.

Effect: This gives managers a sense of superiority, as though only they know the one best way to work safely. It perpetuates the role of managers doing the thinking and workers doing the work. This is the start of the "Park your brains at the door and pick them up before you go home tonight." syndrome. It also reinforces the idea that to improve safety the most important management activity is to focus on motivating workers. This leads to the exclusive use of extrinsic motivation by management to control worker's actions. It eliminates any hope management would allow for or acknowledge the existence of intrinsic motivation.

6. *Four basic methods are available for preventing accidents – engineering revision, persuasion and appeal, personnel adjustment, and discipline.*

Flaw: This is the start of safety management creating a barrier between management and workers. All of these activities are based on the idea that management controls the system and if only the workers would do what they are told their safety would be ensured. It shows no understanding of variation or denies it exists.

Effect: This creates the management vs. workers mentality in safety management. It is the start of simple solutions being offered for the complex problems of safety. Safety management methods are directed at controlling the workers so they will do what management prescribes. When it comes to safety, mangers believe the system isn't the problem. It's the workers, because they don't or won't do what they were told. Eventually this evolves to Three E's of safety, Engineering, Education and Enforcement and the Hierarchy of Controls as **the solutions** to safety problems. Managers with this perspective can't begin to think of workers as customers of safety management.

7. *Methods of most value in accident prevention are analogous with the methods required for the control of quality, cost, and quantity of production.*

Flaw: This really isn't a flaw on Heinrich's part. But all he had to go on at the time was Taylor's approach to management and quality. However, as Taylorism fell out of favor and was replaced by the new quality theories of Deming, Juran, Ohno etc., which stress continual improvement, safety has retained Heinrich's theory with its emphasis on meeting specifications and focusing on the worker to improve safety.

Effect: It opened the door for managers to apply Taylor's methods and theories of scientific management to safety uncritically. As with Taylor, Heinrich's influence is with us today but updated with more modern terms. Until now there has not been a new theory of safety management.

8. *Management has the best opportunity and ability to initiate the work of prevention; therefore it should assume the responsibility.*

Flaw: This was and is a very important point and it wasn't flawed. Unfortunately, it is almost always totally ignored by managers. Heinrich didn't realize that when he said unsafe acts of workers caused most injuries it allowed managers to relinquish their responsibility for safety and they put it squarely on the shoulders of the workers. Once managers did this, they never took it back. In that respect it is flawed.

Effect: Management and managers shun their basic responsibility to design work to be safe in the first place and to improve safety on a daily basis by transferring it to the workers. Managers believe the work systems they provide are perfectly safe. From their point of view all it takes to be safe is a little common sense on the part of the workers. Therefore employees are the ones responsible for their own safety and hence they can be held fully accountable if they are injured. Management believes it has done everything it can when it comes to safety. Consequently workers are at fault when they are injured, not management.

9. *The supervisor or foreman is the key man in industrial accident prevention. His application of the art of supervision to the control of worker's performance is the factor of greatest influence in successful accident prevention.*

Flaw: This gave the power to supervisors and solidified Taylor's command and control system for safety management. Taylor got to the point where he said there should be an enforced cooperation between supervisors and workers. At best this approach strives to maintain the status quo, not continual improvement.

Again it puts the majority of responsibility for accidents on workers by requiring them to follow safety instructions. Any resistance or deviations by the workers to not follow safety rules proves they are not "behaving" safely. It goes back to Taylor's idea that any improvement offered by the worker about the job is "fatal to his success."

Taylor and Heinrich couldn't foresee the onset of knowledge workers, self-directed work teams, hybrid workers and the reduction/elimination of supervision in lean manufacturing.

Modern management requires workers to perform mental as well as manual labor. Taylor never foresaw this happening.

Effect: Prevents supervisors from truly seeking input from workers on whether they believe their job is "safe." Doing so would make the supervisor look weak or not capable of being a supervisor. This creates a barrier between managers and workers.

Supervisors never think of workers as customers of safety. In Heinrich's world, when it comes to safety, workers are actually viewed as the problem. Customers exist both internally and externally but if the supervisor's or foremen's job is to enforce safety they believe they lose power by pandering to employee safety concerns. Given a choice between production and safety, supervisors in this culture chose production almost every time.

10. *The humanitarian incentive for preventing accident injury is supplemented by two powerful economic factors: 1.) the safe establishment is efficient productively and the unsafe establishment is inefficient; 2.) the direct employer cost of industrial injuries for compensation claims and for medical treatment is but one-fifth of the total cost which the employer must pay.*

Flaw: This axiom is not flawed but little attention is paid to it by accountants and management. To this day the calculation of profit never includes the costs of accidents. You don't ever see them in any company's annual report. Why do you think they're called hidden costs?

Effect: The total cost of employee injuries is not known, hence management does not understand the true impact of poor safety performance; not only on the bottom line but on morale and culture. It prevents management from giving the same attention to safety costs as they do to scrap costs.

These 10 Axioms have been applied in many forms and variation since Heinrich created them in 1950. There have been attempts to improve safety management since then but the essence of Heinrich has been sustained. As with Taylor, most managers believe Heinrich's theories have been updated, advanced and replaced by now. The reality is they are still practiced today in a Neo-Heinrich manner. Safety managers will deny they use the negative aspects of Heinrich. In reality most of their activities and routines remain focused on after-the-fact efforts and corrective action as the way to control the frequency of accidents, not prevention. And most of these activities are centered on controlling the behaviors of the workers.

The Taylor/Heinrich legacy in safety

If you break down any traditional safety program you will find it is based on ideas proposed initially by Taylor/Heinrich. They include:

- Personnel
- Safety Rules and Regulations
- Safety training
- Safety inspections/audits
- Accident investigations
- Promotional activities of safety such as incentive programs and rewards
- Focus on employee behavior as the method to prevent accidents

Here is how the current version of the Taylor/Heinrich safety model looks today.

1. Safety has an internal focus with the goal of meeting safety standards mandated by outside Regulators (OSHA, EPA, FDA, etc.) Control of costs for company such as lost time accidents and workers compensation used to evaluate safety improvement actions.

2. Safety is just one of many functional activities of management.

3. Safety is necessary but not considered a competitive advantage.

4. Safety is part of the invisible factory. No way to account for hidden cost or cost of poor safety performance.

5. Safety is treated as a specialized function carried out by a small number of certified experts reporting to Human Resources. Heavy application of extrinsic motivational methods.

6. The downstream focus of safety is to conduct safety inspections, audits, accident investigations and "band-aid" solutions.

7. Safety improvement activities involve repeating the cycle of detect and correct, leading to at best maintaining the status quo.

8. Safety is a stand alone effort handled by the Safety department, not well-integrated with operational activities

9. Safety works independent of other departments and tries to maximize it own goals. Other departments believe safety activities interfere with production time and they see it as an expense item.

All of these activities are designed to help management control the behavior of workers and meet safety specifications that are developed internally by the company or externally by regulators. A great deal of hierarchy and bureaucracy is created with this approach (it certainly can't be considered "lean") just to maintain the status quo. It's expensive, at the very least you have to pay people to administer all of the inspections and audits, which can be argued is not value added work. At best, all it can do is maintain the status quo, at a time when management should be managing for continual improvement of every aspect of the organization. At worst it is used as a crutch by managers not to improve safety but to focus on what workers are doing wrong.

As a result of this approach, many safety managers interpret continual improvement to mean improving what you are already doing, not changing what you do to improve your outcomes. They believe improving the activities listed above, with no change in the purpose of safety management, is what continual improvement of safety is all about.

Part 2

What Do we do wrong

The aim of Part 2 is to show that how we think about safety prevents us from working on making the new model described in the last chapter a reality.

When it comes to safety, why are we so stupid?

Myth: *A popular belief that is false or unsupported by facts*

"Never underestimate the magnitude of the forces that reinforce complacency and help maintain the status quo." John Kotter

Behind every complex question there is a simple answer, and it is wrong! H.L. Mencken

At a two day seminar someone suggested the idea of a Dr. Deming tee shirt. Asked what should be written on it he said: *"Why are we so damn stupid?"*

I've asked hundreds of managers and safety directors a simple question: "What causes employee accidents?"

Their most frequent response is; "Employee carelessness." or; "People not paying attention." Then I show them a formula introduced to me by the safety profession in 1970's. It states:

Unsafe Actions + Unsafe conditions + Time = An accident

I then ask them what causes most accidents, unsafe actions or unsafe conditions? Most choose the latter. When I explain Heinrich's theory that 88% of accidents are caused by the unsafe actions of workers most people nod their heads in agreement. Let's be honest, if you haven't thought about it, his theory is a pretty seductive, rational and logical answer. I had no trouble agreeing with it when I first heard it.

Armed with this information, managers have no need to spend any more time contemplating what causes employee accidents. And who could blame them? They are extremely busy working on the pressing matters of quality and production and Heinrich's theory works well enough for them.

Unfortunately, it doesn't work so well from the employee's perspective. The accident statistics in this country prove it. It was useful in a command and control culture but for continual improvement it leaves a lot of questions unanswered. Like after you have trained employees, protected them from the basic hazards on the job, motivated them to be safe using incentives and rewards and accidents persist, what else is can you do? The answer to that question is, not much.

In his book "Normal Accidents" a study of what causes catastrophic accidents, Charles Perrow says:

"Here we have the essence of a normal accident: the interaction of multiple failures that are not in direct operational sequence....most normal accidents have a significant degree of incomprehensibility." [7]

Perrow admits he is not concerned with the typical run-of-the-mill accidents individual employees have at work. He believes, as most managers still do, more or less mundane precautions and training are all the only things required to prevent them. Unfortunately the methods we use to address everyday run-of-the mill processes can only do so much. The fact is they still result in a lot of people being injured or killed.

Which begs the question, if you are responsible for someone else's safety, as all managers are, and the theory you have about what causes accidents isn't sufficient, how are you supposed to prevent them? To paraphrase Deming, when it comes to safety, why **are** we so stupid?

You would think after all this time we would have a definitive answer to the question, what causes employee accidents? Or at least one that would achieve only 3.4 injuries per million hours worked, not the 4.4 per two hundred thousand hours that happens now. (The industrial revolution started around 1760 and the study of modern safety management began well over a hundred years ago.)

The accident statistics cited at the beginning of this book show that training people, taking ordinary precautions and incentive programs isn't enough. If the answer is known we haven't done much with it. Think about the progress of management in the last one-hundred years relative to quality and productivity. You have to wonder, why hasn't safety advanced as much? The answer is we are using an outmoded paradigm to manage it. We now have a lot of safety problems it does not solve.

We have been using a Newtonian view of the world in safety to try and understand what causes accidents. In this approach to understanding things cause and effect are close in time and space. It's believed all you have to do is look for the one specific thing that misbehaved and you have found the "root cause" of the problems. The theory of learning is all things are discernable. But their Newtonian view of the universe has been turned upside down with quantum theory. We've come to learn that cause and effect are not so closely connected in time and space. In fact there are invisible influences and connections that exist across time and space.

Scientists call this invisible relationship "action-at-distance" and have shown it to exist between two paired electrons. When two paired electrons are separated they will continue to act as one unified electron. Scientist can measure the spin of each electron. If they observe one to spin up the other paired electron will spin down or if one is observed to spin right, the other will spin left. This reality applies to understanding why things happen in daily experience, including things that go wrong such as accidents. There is an invisible interconnectedness in systems

Deming exposed a major fallacy managers held about mass production by posing a simple question to them. When you improve quality, what happens to your costs? The answer most managers gave exposed the weakness in American business. In the 1980's most American managers believed if you worked to improve quality costs went up. They believed this because they could see the connection between all the extra inspection and effort required in their system to make good parts and the extra costs these entailed. For them the two things were close in time and space.

In fact just the opposite is true. Improve quality, costs go down and productivity goes up. The reason is simple; with high quality you have little or no scrap! But they could not see this connection because they did not know how to reduce scrap without adding more costs to their processes in the form of inspections. In addition if your system doesn't produce scrap there literally is nothing to see. The effect of lower costs is there but from their viewpoint American managers couldn't see it.

Deming also had a different explanation as to what causes accidents at work. He said:

> *"Special and common causes. A fault in the interpretation of observations, seen everywhere, is to suppose every event (defect, mistake, accident) is attributable to someone (usually the nearest one at hand), or is related to some special event. The fact is most troubles with service and production lie in the system. Sometimes the fault is indeed local, attributable to someone on the job or not on the job when he should be. We shall speak of faults of the system as common causes of trouble, and faults from fleeting events as special causes."* [8]

This statement contradicted everything I was taught about safety management. The concept of common and special causes as faults that cause accidents creates a very different perspective about safety. Intuitively, it made sense but it took some serious thinking before I understood it. The more I examined his theory the more sense it made.

I realized the same relationship between quality and productivity applies to safety. Improve safety, costs go down and productivity goes up. The reason; no accidents! You cannot have high productivity without high quality and high safety. I found my safety colleagues acknowledge his concepts but would have little or nothing to do with them once they realized it required them to change their methods and their minds.

Deming's way is a totally new approach of how to manage. As a result of applying his theory I became more of a systems thinker. My colleagues seemed more comfortable with single event thinking. I was moving away from being satisfied with the status quo and they couldn't let it go. They were victims of paradigm paralysis which occurs when a paradigm is so strongly held by someone they cannot accept the new one.

Paradigm paralysis occurs when the old way of thinking cannot solve new problems that arise. At that point we start to make up explanations about why things go wrong. These end up being myths but they are treated as being factual.

Safety Myths

One of the reasons people have difficulty changing their views about safety is their strong reliance on faulty assumptions which I call safety myths. Myths are ideas we believe are true but have little or no basis in fact. Here are some I've heard and seen practiced over the years.

Safety Myth number 1 –*When it comes to safety if workers would just do what they're told to do they would not get injured.*

To this I say, sweet dreams. It is similar to the idea that meeting specifications is the way to achieve quality. Meeting specifications used to be "good enough." This approach was OK in the 1950's but it won't work in today's economy. It shows a total lack of understanding about what causes accidents. It is linked directly to Heinrich's theory that unsafe actions are the main cause of employee accidents. No instructions can cover all of the situations workers will encounter. Because of variation, there will always be unanticipated exposures and hazards.

In a culture where employees are always expected to do what they're told, people will eventually lack the ability or enthusiasm to think on the job. So at the very moment when it is most important for them to be thinking about what they are doing, it won't happen. The system has compelled them to do just the opposite. You end up with employees giving you what is called *malicious obedience*. Employees will do only exactly what they are told, no more and no less. This leads to all kinds of problems. They cannot adapt or adjust for all of the various situations they face on the job. And don't think for a minute that standardized work controls this. It does not. There is always variation, even when work is standardized.

Safety myth number 2 – *All accidents can be prevented*

The idea that all accidents are preventable results from looking at a situation from only one perspective, backward. When looking back on an accident you can always say there were things that could have been done to prevent it. Hindsight is always 20/20. The problem is systems are too complex and filled with so much variation it is impossible to know everything that is going wrong or can go wrong before the accident takes place. The statement, 'All accidents are preventable,' has a nice ring to it. It infers you can do something to prevent every single accident *before* they happen, but this just isn't true. The idea comes from people applying non-systems single event thinking to systems consisting of multiple non-sequential events.

There are situations where you can look at something and it is obvious an accident is going to happen, for example a slippery floor. But, there a many other accident producing situations which are not obvious before the accident occurs. If the factors that cause an accident are "incomprehensible" as Perrow says, how can one prevent it?

If you are dealing with an isolated situation, not a system, it seems logical you could prevent the same thing from happening again. The problem is, although work is a constant cause system and processes are repeatable they are never exactly the same. There is always some variation. It may be so small as to not make a difference but it exists nonetheless. A small amount of variation in one or more areas can have an impact much later in time that can directly or indirectly cause an accident. In addition all systems keep changing. That is why no system can be completely free of accidents. Variation and degradation of the system prevent it from happening.

The Taylor/Heinrich management model denies or ignores variation. It focuses on command and control to stop things from going wrong. It's more of a safety by fiat approach. There has been no scientific evidence to prove that all accidents can be prevented. There is plenty of evidence to contradict it. Everyone would like to be accident free. It is always the goal no matter what paradigm you are using. But since we live in an always changing imperfect world it just doesn't happen.

Safety myth number 3 – *Employees come to work to injure themselves*

In over thirty years of interviewing thousands of employees I've yet to find one employee who willfully and knowingly set out to get injured at work. They may be out there but they sure aren't talking. They would be the extreme exception to the rule. Strangely enough, I've met many managers who in their minds believe this statement to be true for the majority of employees. Believe it or not, some managers I've talked with estimate the number of people who come to work to get injured to be as high as ninety per cent! Can you imagine working for a manager with such a low opinion of his employees?

Safety myth number 4 – *If an employee, department, division, or company can make it through one day without an accident, it can make through every day without an accident.*

This statement shows some people don't understand that absence of a negative doesn't mean you have a positive. You can beat horses and they will run faster but only for awhile. Eventually their ability to sustain maximum capacity breaks down, the system catches up with them and they have to slow down. It's the same with accidents. People can and do take precautions to avoid hazards but the system and the faults in it will usually prevail. (People who believe myth #4 may also believe accidents are the result of faith, chance, luck, hope and magic.)

Safety myth number 5 – *The best way to prevent accidents is to conduct a complete and thorough accident investigation with corrective action duly noted and taken on every single accident.*

The thinking here is, if an employee is injured it must be due to something special or unusual at the moment and spot where the accident happened. The belief is you can determine exactly what went wrong and remind the employee not to let that happen again.

Accident investigations are the ultimate example of management driven by single event thinking. By conducting the investigation they believe they are being proactive. The fact is, accident investigations are 100% reactive. They always take place *after* the accident. The investigations are perfect examples of misapplication of cause and effect single event thinking. The problem is cause and effect is not always closely related in time and space. Examining what was going on at the time of an accident almost always ignores or excludes related causes that happened days, months, in some cases even years, before the accident occurred. There are unseen causal relationships that exist in all work systems. It is extremely difficult or even impossible to see or trace the relationship but its influence exists nonetheless.

I know people who conduct accident investigations are really trying to help. (I've done a lot of them myself over the years.) Unfortunately, because of their training, the process has a built-in a bias of looking for the unsafe action (88%) which prevents systems thinking from being applied in the process. There is ample evidence that investigating every single accident has little or no effect on overall safety performance. (Deming noted many quality departments investigating every single defect for years with no improvement in quality. I can report the same results for employee accidents.)

It would be better to do nothing than to conduct an investigation with the unspoken and misguided intent of blaming someone for causing it. This isn't to say you don't examine an accident, but it is better to do so armed with profound knowledge. At least then you will be able to examine what happened with a holistic view and identify faults in the system that led to the accident. Using this approach you will come to understand that in most cases unsafe actions are really symptoms not causes of accidents.

Safety myth number 6 – *Obtaining a safety award or certification ensures safety of employees*

Seeking an award or recognition is more a self-serving activity by management to get a pat on the back than to truly improve safety. Awards have little or nothing to do with daily management and leadership that create the culture required to work on continual improvement of safety every single day. They may make people feel good when they receive them but they won't improve a safety program. (They can also make people feel bad when they don't receive them.) This isn't to say you shouldn't celebrate safety, just don't fall into the trap of thinking that because you got an award things will be OK in the future.

Safety myth number 7 – *One way to ensure and improve safety is to conduct safety inspections.*

It's been known for years that you can't inspect quality into parts or service. The same holds true for safety. You cannot inspect safety into your system. All the safety that exists is in the system when a safety inspection is conducted. Just like quality, a system cannot exceed the amount of safety that was designed and built into it. Your time is much better spent learning how to study and fix or improve the system.

Safety myth number 8 – *Improving safety adds to the cost of production and service*

It is true that a lot of time, effort and money must be spent on leading and managing safety. It's also a fact the payback cannot be accounted for using Generally Accepted Accounting Principles. Operating any work system accident free over time always pays off. The problem is, when safety is perfect this number is always "0." Adding a zero to the bottom line profit is of no interest to top management or accountants.

Look at any Annual Report and see if you can find the numbers for employee accident costs. Where are the numbers for lost productivity when employee accidents occur? What about the numbers for the lack of respect for management? They don't exist. It's been said safety doesn't cost it pays. We just haven't figured out how to produce numbers to account for the impact it has on the bottom line. The impact is there but not accounted for which adds to the crisis poor management creates.

Safety myth number 9 – *Motivating workers to act safely is an important management activity. Get their motivation right and employees will be safe. Using safety incentive programs is an appropriate method to keep employees interested and on-their-toes to watch out for safety problems.*

A lot of companies and managers have spent a lot of money on safety posters directed at workers to remind them to work safely. It's totally unnecessary. Every human being has intrinsic motivation to come to work, do a good job and go home without being injured. Management always couples motivation of workers with holding them accountable for their own accidents thus relieving management of its responsibility for safety. Management's job should be to remove the de-motivators at work that prevent people from being able to work safely at all times. This includes error inducing systems and the use of fear.

Generally, safety incentive programs are the last bag of tricks management uses to improve safety performance. If accidents persist after management has tried everything it knows, they roll out an incentive program. There is overwhelming evidence rewards destroy intrinsic motivation. People possess plenty of intrinsic motivation to be safe at work. Why eliminate it by rewarding them for something they will gladly do in the first place? This is called overjustification.

Management believes employees can be motivated to work safely by offering up a goodie; do this (don't have an accident) and you'll get that (some type of reward). It's a demeaning and deplorable example of management not knowing how to solve a problem and resorting to bribing people. Although their intentions are good the long term consequences are often quite bad. Do people work for rewards? Absolutely. But the consequences of using rewards aren't worth it. People end up working for and expecting rewards. When they stop, and they always do, people's interest in safety stops also. Working for rewards destroys the intrinsic motivation all people have to work safe and do a good job.

The problem with safety rewards is the workers aren't given something else to choose from regarding safety. Imagine workers thoughts if management said, "Would you like to have a safety incentive program with a chance to win a prize or have the shop cleaned up, guards put in place and receive better safety training?"

Safety myth number 10 – *Safety is everyone's responsibility. Workers must be held accountable for safety.*

Managers who believe also this believe the most effective way to improve a person's performance is to remind them about their mistake so they won't do it again. How else will they learn? The principle here is; hold people accountable for things they can control. These managers don't understand that a lot of things done wrong or poorly are mostly the fault of the system.

Top management is ultimately responsible for safety and they can't pass this on to the workers. In the command and control model (Taylor's world) of management, workers have little or no input about the design, management and deployment of safety. Management must always live up to its ethical, moral and legal obligations first. Leadership for safety cannot be delegated to the hourly worker.

For example, employees don't create nor can they improve the quality of safety training they receive. They can't change a culture that creates error inducing processes that has employees forgetting about safety at the very moment it should be a top priority. They don't control the system of budgeting and changing work processes to improve safety. The positive or negative outcomes of all of these activities rest with top management and they are the cause of 85-99% of all accidents in any work system. This responsibility cannot be denied or abdicated.

There is a paradox here. Management cannot relinquish its responsibility for safety but the activities of improving safety can and should and can be performed by everybody in an organization. Workers cannot contribute to improving the system in a command and control Taylor/Heinrich modeled organization. There are too many barriers to prevent it. But they can certainly contribute in a positive constructive culture that manages for continual improvement.

It should be noted there is a difference between divided and joint responsibility. When you have divided or shared responsibility then no one is responsible. They are not connected. Divided responsibility is when an employee is supposed to do something and his supervisor checks up on him to see that he's done it. In this case if one party does not perform their duty they can use the excuse they thought the other party was doing it.

The secret to resolving a mistake by people is to let them be responsible for things they can control. It makes no sense to add another step to a process, like checking on someone, when an employee can do the job correctly without it. Taking a shared responsibility step out reduces anxiety and complexity and keeps the system simple. Adding this step in reduces trust and respect between management and workers.

Joint responsibility is different than shared responsibility. When you have joint responsibility each party's action is required and connected to achieve the overall goal. There is a joint effort between people. Two people that cosign a loan are jointly responsible. A teacher and student are jointly responsible for learning. The teacher must do her job and the student must do his so he can learn how to learn which is the overall goal of the relationship.

Each one of these myths reinforces management's belief there is a simple, easy answer to the question, what causes employee accidents? Every one of them causes damage to management's stature and effort to truly improve safety. The negative multiplying effect of two or more of them prevents understanding of how to manage safety effectively. Taking safety to a higher requires more than relying on myths.

The use of common sense for safety management

Common sense is the collection of prejudices acquired by age eighteen.... Albert Einstein

Common sense is always wrong. Taiichi Ohno

Better not to investigate the truth at all then to do so without a method. Rene Descarte

I would not give a fig for the simplicity this side of complexity but I would give my life for the simplicity on the other side of complexity. Oliver Wendell Holmes

Common sense, where would we be without it? The fact is, where common sense works it serves us rather well. Most of us don't consciously think about how we'll get through each day without having an accident and most days we are successful. In many ways being safe is really just a matter of using our plain old "common sense." By definition, everyone has it. As a result we really don't have to think to hard about working and playing safely. For the most basic circumstances it just comes naturally.

Generally speaking, common sense serves us well when it comes to simple, uncomplicated problems of being safe. It doesn't take much to learn that if you put your hand on a hot stove you'll get burned. Almost everyone learns and understands that at a very early age. But for all its benefits common sense has its drawbacks. Work systems can be filled with hazards that take more than common sense to understand, evaluate and control or eliminate. Even simple work systems are very complex. That means they require higher levels of thinking to comprehend and go about solving them

I've heard many safety managers say, "All it takes for safety is for employees to use their common sense." They are not doing the employees any favors when they approach safety with this attitude.

In a recent newspaper column about why employees don't take part in office fire drills willingly, the author made an interesting observation; *"There's no shortage of people in any office who will claim that missing a deadline or failing to prepare a great PowerPoint presentation has life-or-death consequences. But when it comes to preparing for potentially life-threatening emergencies at work, many of us variously mock the fire marshal, ignore the hair-raising sirens, or assume it's a false alarm."* [9]

I find it interesting that when it comes to solving the problems in any manufacturing process, management realizes it requires a much higher level of reasoning and logic than common sense. Employees receive special training about the scientific method, Design of Experiments, Failure Modes Effect Analysis or a new way of managing such as TQM or Six Sigma. But when it comes to solving safety problems, common sense is deemed totally adequate. Management assumes it is all you need to avoid accidents at work. The fact is common sense isn't a problem solving skill at all. Management doesn't seem to understand safety problems range from simple to very complex and often require much higher level of problem solving skills than just plain old common sense.

When you say someone has common sense you are saying something favorable about him. But when you are talking about solving problems the expression has a less honorific connotation. Common sense is a term to describe literally "beliefs that are common"—common to all men, or arriving from an overall consensus. All people, from the illiterate to geniuses call red things "red," hot things "hot." Common sense is the most basic beliefs obtained over time. We obtain it from experience through our senses and it is the simplest form of reasoning. It's acquired by chance not by virtue of any method. You obtain it literally just by being alive. There's nothing wrong with that and we are all lucky to have it.

But managers who believe all you need for a successful safety program is to apply common sense truly demean safety management. Almost every company proclaims safety as its number one priority for every employee. But when top management presumes that all it takes to run the safety department is common sense safety is often afforded much less stature in the organization. Very seldom does the safety department have a direct line responsibility to the president of a company. Why should it? When she's been told that all it takes to run a safety program is basic common sense. Heck a fifth-grader could do it.

The fact is, when top management believes all you need to manage safety is common sense they are going to give it much less respect and attention than other departments. To begin with, in their eyes safety isn't a money-maker so they don't want to be bothered with it on a daily basis. Therefore it is relegated to a significantly lesser role in the company. (Until there is a major accident/catastrophe or major fine by a regulator then top management quickly elevates the stature of the safety department. They usually seek to have the head of the guilty party that causes the problem on a platter.) Consequently the safety department in many companies often reports to or is part of the Human Resources department.

Heinrich explained he merely adapted the principles of production of his day (created by Taylor) to improve safety. At the time this approach made sense and his methods are practiced to this day. Today's safety manager methods and activities are almost exactly what Heinrich prescribed in 1950. Their time is spent:

- Conducting or administering safety inspections and audits to ensure compliance with safety rules and regulations
- Setting up programs for employee behavior observations to remind employees about working safely (Heinrich's technique wasn't as specific as modern behavior based programs; he just theorized that unsafe acts were the leading cause of employee accidents.)
- Completing or training others to complete accident investigations and take corrective action; usually consisting of retraining workers about safety rules and regulations
- Gathering and analyzing safety data to rank divisions, plants and departments; setting up competition between them
- Negotiating with managers of the divisions, plants and departments on how much of a percentage they will reduce accidents in the next quarter or year.
- Overseeing mass safety training programs mandated by regulators
- Designing and administering incentive programs to motivate workers to work safely

The chart below shows you get the most benefit of safety by planning for it before a process starts. As work proceeds you can try to improve safety but this is very difficult to do. When production is running it will almost always take precedence over safety. After production has been running and is stabilized more time should be spent on improving safety. Unfortunately this is rarely the case.

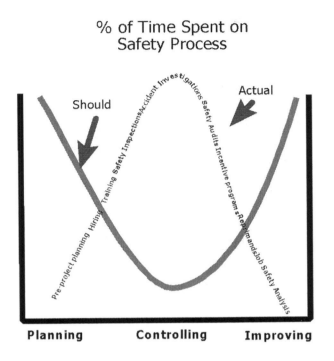

% of Time Spent on Safety Process

Time allocation for safety management

Top management and safety managers spend their time controlling safety. It's what they understand best. If safety managers were not allowed to conduct safety inspections, audits, and incentive programs they would have an enormous amount of free time on their hands. They wouldn't know what else to do.

To take safety to a higher level requires more than just common sense. The problem is we spend a lot of time and effort on other activities that don't add much value to safety management.

Meeting specifications through safety inspections

Most safety management activities are done to ensure operations comply with safety specifications. These come in the form of company safety rules or legal safety requirements (OSHA, EPA, etc.) To find out if safety specifications are being met means conducting extensive safety inspections and audits.

It has been known for over fifty years that final inspections are an ineffective method for improving quality. Quality management started to understand this in the 1950's when people began to realize the deficiencies of inspections for quality control.

Basically you don't get ahead by making product, performing inspections then separating the good from the bad. Doing so costs a lot of money and you seldom get around fixing what caused the bad parts in the first place. You cannot inspect quality into your product or service. If you want to improve quality you should spend more time and effort building quality into each process so final inspections aren't necessary. The fact is you can't inspect safety into your operations either. Some of the problems with safety inspections are:

- They take the focus away from the system and put it on single events and symptoms
- They are always too late. The amount of safety that exists in a process cannot be increased by conducting an inspection.
- They are just a snapshot and are only good for the time and place they are conducted. Processes have variation so they are constantly changing.
- Any two inspectors will produce different results.
- The unwritten but underlying message conveyed when conducting inspections is; employees can't be trusted to do the job right. Therefore management must inspect operations for problems created by the inattention or inability of employees and take corrective action on that single person.
- They're expensive. Someone has to be paid to conduct them, document them, analyze them and follow up and do them again.
- Their existence perpetuates the myth that doing something is better than doing nothing.
- You cannot see everything during an inspection so you will always miss something. Inspections will not help you see the invisible elements of the system.
- They're designed to tell you what has been done wrong but they can't tell you how to fix it.

It is easy to see inspections are not the most effective way to improve the safety of any process or system.

Audits are just another form of inspections. They're done to ensure a process "meets safety specifications." Managing to meet specification ensures no continual improvement will take place for two reasons. First, the goal when conducting a safety inspection is to maintain the status quo. Second, as long as you meet specifications that's "good enough": it doesn't matter how much variation exists. Indeed it is very difficult to even decide what the limits are for most safety specifications. For example, when you test people on their knowledge about power lockout after they've been trained, at what point do they meet specifications? Is it ok for them to achieve a test score of 80%? 70%? Or must everyone get 100%?

Safety professionals have interpreted continual improvement as meaning to improve their existing safety management methods. They honestly believe improving the quality and quantity of safety inspections and audits equates to improving safety. The only thing that will happen is they will discover even more variation and not be able to do anything about it, making matters worse. It's been said that anything not worth doing is not worth doing well. For all the reasons noted above, safety management should cease dependence on mass safety inspections/ audits.

Benchmarking and best practices

Searching for best practices of safety and health programs by benchmarking and trying to duplicate them will not help you achieve continual improvement of safety either. Basically I've found managers use benchmarking as an excuse to get away from their own operations for awhile. One large manufacturer I know had its corporate safety staff spend almost two years benchmarking other companies. When it was completed no major changes were implemented.

One big problem with benchmarking is; who determines what a "best practice" is for safety? I attended a safety conference at which a presenter on the topic of best practices stated his company believed it was all about getting employees involved. He said; "Employee involvement provides the means through which workers develop and express their own commitment to safety." I have never met anyone who was not committed to their own safety. He then explained the methods for obtaining employee involvement were to have safety committees, safety contests and incentive programs. They just wanted people to be more aware of their surroundings and be more careful. Nothing was offered to change or improve the system.

The presenter then proceeded to say control of hazards in the workplace is best done by conducting safety inspections and/or audits. Another company presented a program in which employees go out and observe other employee's safety behavior and reward them for working safely. The intention was to provide "positive feedback" to workers. This could hardly be considered any kind of profound insight about best practices of safety management. I couldn't help but think this was the same advice I heard thirty years ago at a similar safety conference.

In the 1980's American managers tried to copy the quality circles they saw when they visited Japanese companies. It didn't work. They did not understand that quality circles were connected to a larger quality system. Without the knowledge of how they fit with the larger system, copying them was a useless exercise. They brought back the things they could see and tried to use them. Just having employees sit around in a circle and talk about quality problems doesn't mean you are fixing any of them. They missed the important things you can't see about quality circles that truly make them work such as a constructive culture and systems thinking. Without these quality circles didn't have a chance.

The same is true for safety. Even if you could find a best practice for safety in a company, trying to copy it won't do you any good. Your situation will never be exactly the same as the one you are trying to mimic. You will eventually have to deal with reality in your operations.

To a single event thinker these well intentioned programs sound good. Unfortunately, they provide nothing in the way of continual improvement of safety management. But how could they know? They were only concerned with events, the things you can see.

Meeting safety specifications and ignoring variation is no longer 'good enough.' Taking safety to a higher level will require more. Benchmarking, observing someone else's safety program and trying to emulate it will not provide the answer.

Negative effects of Taylorism/Heinrich on safety

There are some negative management activities Neo-Taylor/Heinrich has on current safety management:

Managers need to control things

- Job safety analysis is done by experts off-line who don't work in the system and use standards that apply to the average worker. It's assumed this creates the best design to eliminate accidents.
- Managers and workers never use or know what an operational definition is so they don't determine whether or not the job is safe. Managers use their definition of "safe."
- Managers use a line of reasoning to persuade employees they are solely responsible for safety which basically relieves management from its responsibility to work on improving the system.

The emphasis placed on documentation of safety activities instead of improving work process.

- Safety training focused on telling employees what not to do so they won't get hurt instead of helping them learn how to learn and solve the safety problems they encounter in production.
- No way of learning if people grasp and retain what they've learned from safety training that is administered.

Employing competition within the company

- Measuring and comparing the accident records of individual departments, locations, branches, plants, etc. in an effort to motivate one to be better than the other which leads to demoralizing the workforce.

Believing there is one main cause of accidents: people

- Management schemes to make workers work safely. Contests, incentive programs, positive reinforcement of catching a worker doing his job safely and rewarding him. None of these ever made the system safer.
- No understanding or thought given to the negative and destructive affect of exclusive use of extrinsic motivators
- Arbitrary safety goals tied to bonus programs as if workers had control of the system that produces accidents. (If you can do it this year without a theory, why didn't you do it last year? You must have been goofing off.)

Use of fear to motivate workers
- Reminding workers how much money is spent on safety
- Punishing workers by using safety incentive programs
- Threatening to shut down a plant because of its poor safety record
- Placing accident investigation reports in personnel files and use them in performance appraisals.

Talking about culture and how it impacts safety but doing nothing to learn how to do anything about it, e.g. measure it, change it, improve it and sustain it
- Belief that an organization has only one culture, no sub-cultures.
- Failure to obtain and apply profound knowledge to create a positive culture in the organization

- Ignorance and disregard of how systems impact the actions of individuals.
- Individual workers efforts recognized, not teams. This is true for the incentive programs and heroic efforts of people being depended on by management to work without getting injured.
- Double deception of employees through safety empowerment and teams that work on solving safety problems but have to submit the solutions to management for their approval, only to have them rejected with a dubious explanation or excuse as to why it can't be done.
- Management says safety is no. 1. Little evidence can be produced to support this claim and a lot can be found to refute it, e.g. minimal budget for safety training and new equipment, safety meetings canceled, top management doesn't attend safety meetings, change in attitude of management toward safety depending upon the latest safety performance, laying off safety personnel when business is slow, etc.
- No true way for workers to contribute to improving safety on-the-job.

Viewing workers as bionic machines
- Failure to recognize or understand the effect the safety management system (or lack of) has on the individual worker. From the day a person starts working for a company what are the effects of poor safety management in the form of

weak or limited safety training geared only to meeting safety regulations/specifications.

- Managers and engineers don't have to experience the physical toll of what it's like to do a job for 8 hours a day, 5-6 days a week, 50 weeks a year. Consequently they have no empathy for the physical and mental hardship of what the hourly workers face on their jobs.

- Departments that have no idea about what is actually going on at workstations yet they are allowed to make policy that impacts safety of these operations. This includes purchasing, engineering, finance and human resources.

- No way to adjust the process once production starts. If you are 5' 2" or 6' 5" it doesn't matter. You must work at the job whether you fit or not.

Part 3

The new start

The aim of Part 3 is to introduce profound knowledge and how Deming's 14 Points should be applied to safety management. Profound knowledge is a new way to view an organization to help put things into focus. The 14 Points are a new paradigm of safety management.

> *A traveler lost, seeking help, stops and asks a local 'How do you get to Silver Mountain?' After a few moments pondering the question, the local mountain man replies, 'If I were going to Silver Mountain, I wouldn't start from here.'*
> "*The difficulty lies not in the new ideas, but escaping from the old ones.*"
> John Maynard Keynes, British Economist

Profound Knowledge

> *Dr. Deming's philosophy and that of neo-Taylorism, are locked in a battle for control of management in the Western world—yet few realize this.* [10]

> *We've lost count of the number of senior executives who have told us that adopting the Deming philosophy was the best and hardest thing they had ever done.* [11]

Profound knowledge is a system to study the world around us and the systems we work in. It will help you apply the 14 points of safety management discussed later. Don't let the term scare you. "Profound" implies something deep and mysterious but having a basic understanding of the concept is all that is necessary to reap the benefits of it. Profound knowledge provides a new way to look at your organization and gain a better understanding of how to optimize it. It is a new way of thinking about systems and consequently a fundamental requirement for good management.

To make the transformation from command and control to team management, managers must be able to see and do things differently. Management, its structure and purpose has to be transformed to meet the challenges of the 21st century. Profound knowledge will help you better understand and deal with any organization.

The four points of profound knowledge

Profound knowledge provides an outside view of an organization. You don't need a formal advanced education to understand and practice it. The transformation of an individual is the first step in profound knowledge. Once a person learns and understands profound knowledge it will transform how they look at life, events, numbers and interactions between other people. The more people in your organization who acquire profound knowledge the more it will be able to improve.

The four areas of the system of profound knowledge are: [12]

- Appreciation for a system
- Knowledge about variation
- Theory of knowledge
- Psychology

How to improve systems through the lens of Profound Knowledge

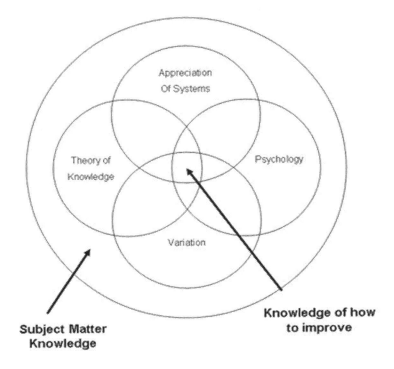

Profound Knowledge

Work systems cannot understand themselves and they certainly won't get better on their own. To improve a system takes people who have a special insight and understanding to critically analyze what is going on. This unique ability is what profound knowledge is all about. Deming believed people who learn and practice profound knowledge will;

Set an example
Become a good listener, but will not compromise
Continually teach other people
Help people change their paradigms about things without feeling guilty about the past
Be a lifelong learner

Systems

When placed in the same system, people, however different, tend to produce similar results. Peter Senge

The first point in profound knowledge is to start to think about and understand systems. Years ago I attended a seminar about management in which the instructor defined a system as: "A series of events set up to accomplish a goal." As far as it goes it is a pretty good definition. But it doesn't quite do justice to the term.

Most of the time we visualize a system operating in an orderly, sequential progression; step one, then step two and so on. Heinrich actually used a series of dominoes standing on end falling sequentially in the same direction one by one to show how each step in a system is directly connected to the next. This single event thinking dominates how we see the structure of systems. We've used it so often and so long it is now a habit. Subconsciously, it's how we think about systems.

This thinking has led us to believe the best way to understand a system is to break it down and study each individual part separately from the others. When we do this we come to the logical conclusion that a system is the sum of its parts. As a result we assume the best way to get the optimal performance from a system is to maximize each part. In an organization this means each department works as hard as it can. Production makes all the parts it can every shift. Purchasing does all it can to reduce costs on every transaction, etc. There is plenty of evidence to show this does not reap the best performance from a system. If fact, quite often it results in 1+1+1+1 equaling 2.

In this type of culture when someone from one department asks someone from another department for help they will often be told, "Its' not our job!" People who work in this type of organization do not understand, nor do they care if the parts of the system work together for the benefit of the whole. They worry only about how well they are doing individually. Each part of the system has no problem trying to outdo the other. This is exactly what happens in a command and control management system. Managers often refer to departments as "silos" when they describe departments in this type of organization.

To gain a better understanding of what a system is, we need a more precise, detailed definition. Deming says a system is a network of interdependent components that work together to accomplish an aim. Without an aim you would just have a bunch of processes working willy-nilly by themselves for their own benefit. So a system must have a purpose, a reason as to why it exists.

Let's add some more details about systems.

Systems have three defining characteristics: [13]

1. *A system does not exist only for itself. It functions to serve a larger whole other than itself.* Your doctor's office exists so you can go there and be treated by your doctor. It is part of the health care system. A school is a building where teaching and learning takes place and is a system but it is also part of a larger educational system. The safety department is a system and exists to educate, inform and train people about solving safety problems at work. It is part of a corporation which produces a product or service which is a system that serves society as a whole.

2. *Every system must have at least two essential parts without which it cannot perform what it was designed to do.* For example, the production and safety departments in a manufacturing plant or nurses and physicians in a hospital. Each is an essential part of the system but it must have at least one other essential part or a system would not exist. Without an essential part the system would not function properly. Remove the heart, lungs or brain and the human system won't work. Remove the safety function from manufacturing and the system won't work properly.

3. *Each essential part of the system can affect the system as a whole but the way one of these parts affects the whole depends on the behavior of the other essential parts. This means no essential part has an independent effect on the system. Each one interacts directly or indirectly with each other.* For example the way a safety department affects the safety performance of a company depends on its interactions with the other departments such as production, shipping and receiving, not what it does on its own. If the safety department

and production do not cooperate, collaborate, communicate and work well together, then safety and productivity in operations will not be optimized. Safety performance is not based solely on how the safety department does its job but also on its interactions with other departments.

We tend to think of a system as a series of well-defined steps taken in a straight line. In reality, systems, even simple ones, are often quite complicated, complex and anything but orderly. Some things take place while others are waiting to fulfill their purpose. For example you might train employees on an essential safety topic one day and they don't use the information for weeks or months later.

There are two types of complexities in systems. When there are a lot of variables it is called detailed complexity. The second type is called dynamic complexity, where cause and effect are subtle and the effects over time are not so obvious. For example, a person may not be required to use power lock out for some time after being trained about it. Consequently he may forget some details about it. These complexities make systems, even simple ones, extremely difficult to study, improve and control.

We can understand systems better by understanding the interactions between the parts as opposed to taking them apart and examining and studying them separately. Systems are wholes defined by the product of the interactions of the parts not the sum of the parts. When you separate the parts you lose the ability to understand the system. Taken apart the system will not function as it is meant to, seriously limiting your ability to see how it works when everything is connected.

In business there can be instances when one part of a system should take a loss so the overall performance of the system gains. For instance, the purchasing department may have to pay more for a piece of equipment that will make the job safer and easier for the workers. Over the long run this will ultimately reduce accidents and costs which will improve overall productivity and morale. Purchasing may lose on their immediate goal of reducing the cost of every single transaction but the company gains because total costs, which include safety, productivity and morale, are reduced. In this case a small negative ends up producing a big positive.

You cannot get 100% efficiency from a system. There is always some amount of waste. Waste includes time, motion, overproduction, material, missed opportunities for improvement and employee injuries. There is also waste that can't be seen such as hidden costs of accidents, people not being able to contribute to improve their work, ineffective meetings and fear, just to name a few. In most cases, these hidden costs can't be measured. Some people believe if you can't measure something you can't manage it. This isn't true. Hidden costs may be the most important thing in a system so even though you can't see or measure them you still have to manage them.

How you manage a system depends on how you think about them. This gets a little confusing but essentially it means how you manage a system is a system. That's what all the review of Taylor and Heinrich was all about.

The pictures below show are examples of two types of systems. The first is Taylor's traditional command and control organizational chart used by most companies to manage people and operations. When it was first proposed it was modeled after a biological system also shown but with a major difference. In the command and control model, each department lacks the ability to work cooperatively with the others. It requires no creativity and encourages bureaucracy, the most abusive type of system.

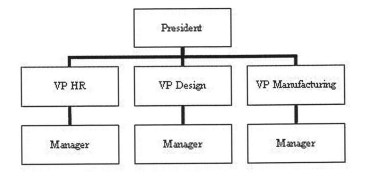

Modern organization chart

The second picture is the biological system of the human body. Each component has a shared purpose of keeping you healthy. It is an autonomic system that monitors and responds to everything happening in the system. The parts work both together and separately depending on what is going on at any given moment. They do not require permission to work together, it just happens naturally. When the parts don't work together as they are supposed to things can go really bad such as when cancer cells occur. The way the biological system functions is becoming the model of management in the 21st century.

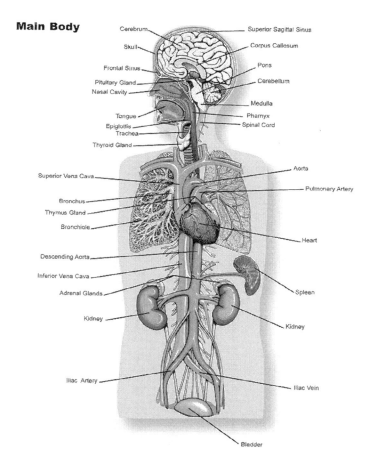

The human body system

Work is actually an artificial system created by people. The main difference between an artificial work system and natural systems is the former is not self-correcting nor self-assembling. When you study systems you realize the parts of a system are interactive, inter-connected, interrelated and interdependent. To be efficient our work systems must be managed and we can manage them any way we choose. There are no pre-ordained laws about how it's done. It's strictly up to us.

Examples of natural systems

- Universe – space
- Weather
- Climate
- Human beings
- Biological
- Quantum

Characteristics of natural systems

- Time
- Self-assembling
- Self-healing
- Can be studied
- Can be understood
- Goal = change and evolve

Examples of artificial systems

- Work
- Play

Characteristics of artificial systems

- Man made
- Do not improve by themselves
- Atrophy over time
- Do not self-assemble
- Must be managed to be efficient
- Have a structure – Interdependent
- Have an order – Interactive
- Have relationships – Interrelated
- Must have an aim, a purpose, a reason for existing

- Have inputs, processes, outputs (sub-systems)
- Can be studied
- Can be understood
- Components do not always have to be clearly defined and documented
- Management needs to understand interactions and interrelationships of parts in the system
- Aim, reason for existing = what you want it to be

Systems thinking

In our task-oriented society, we tend to be habitual, unconscious, single event thinkers. From the Nun and the Bureaucrat[14]

Systems thinking is a relatively new concept in management. Not many people truly understand what it is let alone how to apply it. Most of us apply single event thinking to evaluate a system. This means when we want to understand a system we break it down into its individual parts and study each one separately. This is exactly the opposite of systems thinking. When you do this you are going to miss a great deal about understanding a system.

To truly understand a system you have to be able to see how each part depends on and interacts with the others. Systems thinking is literally a new way of looking at things. It has been described as a revolutionary mindset that gives you a new perspective of how to interact with work, customers and other people.

Most people think a system, like a machine shop or a hospital, is the sum of its parts. They believe that if every person does their job to best of their ability the system will work at maximum efficiency. This single event thinking perspective appears to have worked quite well in the past. In simpler times it was all that was required to understand and manage how work got done.

But with work becoming more complex and demanding, single event thinking will not help management meet the challenges it faces in an always changing, highly competitive world. We will need to look at things differently to make sense of what's going on. That's where systems thinking comes in.

Systems thinking is a new mindset described by Peter Senge as "the discipline of seeing wholes"[15]. It provides the framework to see the interrelationships and patterns that exist in a system. It helps us see that to achieve system optimization each part of the system must cooperate, not compete with the others. Systems thinking helps people understand that internal competition is disastrous to a company and can result in whole organizations with learning disabilities. It also helps everyone understand why their effort makes a difference and how they contribute to the whole.

Rosabeth Moss Kanter, a respected management consultant, says for companies to prosper in the 21st century they will have to become fast, focused, flexible and friendly. Some people in management are beginning to manage more like the biological autonomic nervous system so their company can anticipate and respond to problems locally, be more successful and friendlier. To operate this way will require systems thinking where the whole can produce *synergy* and actually exceed the sum of its parts. In other words, 1+1+1 can equal 4 or more!

Systems thinking for safety management

Accidents, like creativity, are properties of systems rather than of individuals. Mihaly Csikszentmihaly

Command and control has been the predominant approach to manage safety when the ultimate aim is the enforcement of rules and regulations to make people obey them. It works to some extent, but you pay a big price for using it. Basically, you end up stifling the creativity and ingenuity of all of your employees through the uncritical application of bureaucracy and hierarchy. Command and control management with its emphasis on meeting safety standards and maintaining the status quo is the perfect environment for task oriented, single event thinking to thrive.

The primary defense for accidents in command and control is referred to as the Hierarchy of Controls. This plan is set up to identify hazards and control them by; first eliminate them if at all possible and if they can't be eliminated substitute something less hazardous. If hazards can't be eliminated engineering controls are the next option. This typically calls for separating the operator from the hazard or machine guarding. And if these actions aren't adequate the final effort is to have workers use various types of personal protective equipment (PPE). This has evolved into the Three E's of safety management; Engineering, Education and Enforcement.

But in today's economy where continual improvement and reduction of costs are the overarching goals of managing a business, a new way of looking at safety is required. Continual improvement of any type of work system means operations and processes will be changing on almost a daily basis.

This means the status quo for safety management will not be adequate. In this world, safety standards, rules and regulations will have to be defined operationally to be effective. For safety management to be relevant people will have to manage safety through new eyes. Safety managers must learn systems thinking to gain new understanding of what they do, how they do it and who they do it for. It will help them make sense of a complex, constantly changing world.

The reason safety exists in any company should be to answer the question: How will management create a culture to take care of the safety needs of each and every customer (employees) every day? This is a common activity when it comes to quality and it should be for safety. Imagine the enormous gains to be made if companies would take a truly proactive approach to managing safety. People would learn how to work together so accidents are kept at an absolute minimum in all work systems. They would be able to solve the safety problems of dynamic and detailed complexity in their system of hiring, training and putting people to work.

Systems thinking will help people identify, work on and solve what were previously invisible and insoluble problems. Managers would no longer be forced to choose between production and safety. (Most managers will admit when this happens they will choose production first. What else could they do since they can't see the safety problems?)

Systems thinking will also help people address faulty safety rules or regulations that don't relate to actual work conditions. Enforcing safety rules when they do not meet the needs of employees in a particular situation does not guarantee their safety. (See operational definitions.) A single event mindset of 100% adherence to specifications at all times can lead to unresolved conflict between the production and safety department. Systems thinking will result in departments cooperating with each other for the benefit of the workers.

American managers have to learn systems thinking. They will have to work at it consciously. It will be difficult if not impossible for them to think about safety any other way. It won't come naturally. Managers have been relying on the Hierarchy of Controls to handle safety hazards which is an analytical as opposed to a systemic approach.

Using analysis isn't wrong. But if it is the only way you look at something you pay a price of not being able to look for or explain the behavior of a system. Consequently you won't be able to understand how all the parts fit together and how each of them affects the others. You will ignore the dynamics that exist between the parts and how the system you are studying fits into the expanded system in which it serves.

Within these links between the parts are the subtle ways cause and effect are connected. They are not always close in time and space. Most of the time you can't see how they interact but these connections exist and they will impact your system. To ignore them is to do so at your own peril.

For example, engineers are famous for designing work processes without considering how the safety of workers will be affected. Even when they do they seldom look at the operation from the worker's viewpoint. They try to visualize it through their own eyes not someone who will be running the operation 8 hours a day 5 days a week. One reason for this lack of attention to safety is the absence of systems thinking. It's not because they don't care about the workers, they do. But since they are not close to the system (I've seen assembly processes designed by engineers located in different states who never saw the actual work area.) and don't use systems thinking, they tend to view employees as bionic machines that just happen to be paid to work. With this perspective there is no way they can visualize how people interact with the system they are designing.

Absence of systems thinking is also a big part of the reason we have such a hard time fixing systems. For the most part managers, engineers and designers are more task oriented and inclined toward single event thinking. They have no problem with tweaking the system in one area and not thinking about how it will affect other areas, especially when it comes to safety. Systems thinking provides a new set of eyes specifically for this purpose.

The lack of systems thinking is what prevents people from understanding the system itself causes most employee accidents. It's not unusual for engineers to design work systems and leave it to the safety department to figure out how to make things safe after production starts. The inefficiency of this method cannot be understated. In almost every company the safety department has little or no power to make changes once production is underway. Ask anyone who has tried to fix or change a process after production has begun. Does the phrase, "fat chance" mean anything to you?

Some managers will point to times when they have workers examine machinery and give their input about production and safety problems prior to purchasing it and putting it into operation as an example of being proactive. This is a step in the right direction but production design still takes precedence in most cases. And most production operations are in place so continual improvement actions for safety are very limited.

When it comes to safety most companies apply single event thinking with a vengeance and they usually end up with terrible results. Think about how a professional symphony would sound if every member tried to show off their musical talent instead of playing to demonstrate the orchestra's ability. I've seen this attitude often in business when a manager sees an opportunity for profit at the expense of worker's safety. It's what led Heinrich to believe the individual worker could stop accidents if only they would pay closer attention to they are doing. He saw their heroic efforts as the answer to solving safety problems. Systems thinking eliminates the default assumption that an individual is mostly responsible for things going wrong and must be held accountable when something bad happens.

Single event thinkers worry only about themselves and maybe about their individual department, not how their effort influences or impacts someone else or other departments in their organization. They believe in the certainty of cause and effects that are tightly coupled. Cause and effect is an important and relevant concept however they are not always closely related in time and space. But even when they are separated by time and space they remain connected in varying degrees.

We can also see the effect of single event thinking in the desire and need traditional managers have to seek out the "root cause" of an accident. When people lack of ability to understand systems they cannot comprehend that the system itself with all of its variation and interaction caused the accident. Instead, they apply analysis to examine the system and solve problems that come out of it. They break down the accident into separate parts and attempt to determine which one is the *root cause*. Entire books have been written on the subject. System thinking helps one understand that accidents are almost always a result of multiple interacting causes that occur randomly over time.

A person using systems thinking understands accidents are the product of the interactions of the system which creates and controls, or doesn't control, hazards. Work is a system of many different kinds of jobs and each job is a process and sub-processes. They know that how the system performs depends on how well everything in the system works together.

Systems thinking helps you see how the interactions of components of the system result in accidents. With this perspective it's easy to understand why searching for a root cause when you are dealing with an accident created by multiple interactions becomes a fool's errand. Especially when you realize most accidents involve more than one cause. Yet in most instances this is exactly why traditional accident investigations are conducted, to find the root cause.

Systems thinking will help people understand that safety standards must be improved so they will always be effective. The safety system needs to be self-correcting so it can solve these types of problems that exist in every system. This can only happen if we learn and apply systems thinking to examine how we manage safety standards at work.

Systems thinking will help people understand how variation creates accidents in work processes. Unless you understand and plan how to manage variation that can cause accidents in your work system, you can really mess things up. Studying variation will help you see if a mistake is built into the system (A Common Cause) and is likely to recur or if it is an unusual event that may never happen again (A Special Cause).

Knowing how to recognize the difference will help prevent you from tampering with the system. (Tampering is when you try to fix the system when you would be just as well off if you left it alone.) If you know how to determine if the mistake is in the system and has to be fixed, by using an SPC chart for example, you can then take the deep dive and study the system. It's at this point you apply the Plan, Do, Study and Act cycle.

If the mistake is something not likely to ever occur again and you are confident about it, there is no need to take any action. What is done is done and you won't be able to do anything about it anyway. These are what Deming described as special causes and can be handled locally.

Contrast this with traditional management approach which requires action to be taken on every single event no matter where it comes from. Find the cause and fix it. The new way is to determine if the problem is built into the system and has to be solved or if it is outside the system you can just ignore it. Traditional command and control managers just cannot accept any inaction as a proper reaction to trouble.

To become a systems thinker you must constantly work on seeing and understanding wholes. An example of this is the medical field which has learned a lot about the human body and now understands it is much greater than just the sum of its parts. Each part works with the others. The brain, lungs, arms, hands and legs all work together but it's the interactions and connections between them that make up the body so it can do things like walk, write a letter or make the bed. One part not connected to the others will not work on its own. If you cut off your leg it can't get up and walk. It must be connected to the body and all of the components to work properly. The interactions between the parts are what make it work. (You put aspirin in your stomach to relive the pain in your head.)

The new management model must learn to employ systems thinking and function more like the human body. Traditional safety relies on what can be seen to understand the causes of accidents. Actions, such as employee's unsafe actions are visible. They're observable, easy to see and measure. People prone to single event thinking are comfortable in dealing with them. This approach is no longer adequate. It doesn't come close to telling the whole story. It disconnects what you see and other parts of the system you cannot see.

For example, the culture of an organization is invisible so it is very difficult to define and understand. Cause and effect is not always close in time and space which also makes it extremely difficult to see the connection between the two. Yet the interactions, the things you can't see are often the most important things about a system. They are responsible for most of what happens. These invisible connections make a system do what it does. It is where most accidents are created and a systems thinker comprehends this. Single event thinking cannot.

It's that aspect of the system Deming is talking about when he says 85-99% of accidents are built into the system. It explains the conflict with Heinrich, who applies single event thinking, and naturally concludes unsafe actions, which you can see, cause 88% or more of employee accidents.

Command and control management believes it is important to hold someone responsible for things that have gone wrong and take action on a particular person. In the case of an employee injury, you can bet your last dollar that someone, not management, is going to be held accountable. People limited to using single event thinking will direct corrective action exclusively at a person, not the system. The majority of the time their efforts would be misplaced.

Deming also championed what single event thinkers consider to be a ridiculous idea. He said when it comes to improving quality it is silly to conduct a full fledged investigation into every single defect. He cites numerous examples of quality managers and engineers pointing proudly to the fact they investigate every single defect as if it is an important quality technique and the reasons for doing it are self-evident. Then he notes in spite of their Herculean efforts the level of defects in their operations stayed the same or deteriorated over the years. He explains the lack of improvement is because they never get around to identifying and fixing the systemic problems that cause the defects.

History has shown that investigating every single bit of information about a defect or accident does little or nothing to fix the interactions of the system that caused the problem. The reason is the bias built into investigations to separate the parts of the system to perform analysis described earlier and then fix the blame instead of fixing the system.

I can report the same attitude for safety management; companies point proudly to the fact they require supervisors to investigate every single accident yet the average number of accidents is not reduced. Many of the same types of accidents are repeated. How could they improve? These well-intentioned efforts do nothing to fix faults in the system that create the accidents.

Systems thinking helps you recognize when you are merely patching a problem (Putting forth a solution with no testing of the hypothesis.) instead of solving it. Accident investigators often stop at the point where they believe they've found the single thing that caused the accident. There is no way to determine if their conclusion is truly correct.

The truth is managers who use single event thinking spend more time and effort planning for the next accident than preventing them. They believe most accidents are unusual events as though everything else in the system was working correctly up to the moment the accident happened. This approach is void of any type of systems thinking. These managers end up holding employees responsible or accountable for things they can't control. It is difficult if not impossible for continual improvement of safety performance in their world.

Variation

It's a fact of life that no two things are exactly alike. You can see the differences in people, the way they look, act and do things. When it comes to work, variation exists in all areas and at all levels. You can have the same person doing the same job with the same equipment and materials day after day and the results will be different. They may not be immediately perceptible and they may not be enough to matter but they are there. Two or more people doing the same job increases variation even more. You have to learn how to study the variation in a system to learn what effect it has on outcomes.

To improve a system it's a good idea to know how much variation exists in each process. Once you have learned how to measure variation then you can start to work on reducing it. If you don't know how much variation is going on there's no way you will know where it is and what to do about it. You also need to know the predictability of the variation in your processes. If as a manager you don't recognize that variation exists you can and will make expensive and dumb mistakes.

When it comes to safety it's not that difficult to measure variation. For instance the number of accidents every month will vary. By measuring them you can determine if your safety management system is statistically stable, out of control or on target. Depending on which it is determines how you as a manager should react.

Some safety professionals believe an emphasis on measuring accidents shows management isn't being proactive. They miss the point entirely. Deming showed us how using data from the system, even though it may be making defects, leads to taking the correct action on the system which ultimately reduces defects and accidents. You can never eliminate accidents entirely but you will never get around to fixing the system without collecting and using data from it.

To do a better job of managing safety we need to understand variation and how it affects safety performance. Most variation in work exists because of the way the system is managed. For safety that means all of the things you manage such as; safety training, people, materials, methods, machinery and equipment, the environment and culture have variation.

How you lead people and manage the system will have the most influence of how many accidents will occur in your operations. The variation in each part of the system can impact the other parts of the system which can create employee accidents. If a company has employees working that are not following good safety practices, ignoring basic safety procedures or complicated ones for that matter, whose fault is that? There can also be variation outside your system that can impact the number of accidents that will take place.

For instance, approximately 50% of all marriages in the U.S. end up in a divorce. People can and do have a lot of stress in their lives. They may have a seriously ill child at home. At the moment an employee should be thinking about the safety of their work, they might be worrying about things going on in their personal life. Many of them go to work every day with things on their minds that could be serious distractions. I'm quite certain these could be a major contributor to many accidents on-the-job but I have never seen them described in an accident investigation report.

Another impact of variation on safety is the age of the workforce. The U.S. has an aging workforce of the baby boomers. Their physical and mental condition is not what it was when they were in the 20's and 30's. Studies have also shown that as much as 40% of all working age adults report to work every day experiencing some form of sleep deprivation. These are just a few of the external causes of variation that impact the number of accidents in your processes. They are buried in your system out of view. Even the most strident safety inspections will not uncover them. Managers may not like it or even acknowledge it, but they are there and if you are going to improve safety, you will have to find some way of dealing with them effectively.

Accident rates will vary over time. Without an understanding of what the variation means managers are prone to treat each data point as though something unique is going on. If they go up one month they demand to know why. If they go down the next they pat the supervisor or safety manager on the back even though they did nothing to influence the outcome. They give them credit for something over which they may not have any control. The variation may mean nothing at all if the safety in the operations is stable. The problem is, every single data point for accidents is a defect and the target is always zero which means the focus on safety should never be abandoned. Unfortunately, that's what happens when management interprets a single decrease in accidents as a positive and an increase as a negative. (See Statistical Process Control)

Knowledge

The value of an idea lies in the using of it. Thomas A. Edison

Students enter the school system as a question mark wanting to ask and learn and they leave as a period. Neil Postman

Deming was fond of pointing out that experience without theory teaches nothing. Without a theory (a prediction) you have no way of testing your observations. Obtaining knowledge is a continual process of making a prediction then using a theory and testing the theory to find out if what you predicted actually happens. Every time you test your theory and it works you gain more confidence in it. But, by definition you can never prove your theory. There's no way to say the next test of your theory will not produce an anomaly. If it does you must be prepared to modify or abandon it.

This is the learning process of the scientific method. It is a system of observing, asking a question, developing a hypothesis and then testing it to see how it works to give us a way to learn about the world around us. It's not the only way for studying the world but it is a more disciplined, structured form of learning than common sense and intuition. This isn't to say intuition and common sense don't have their place. It's a matter of learning when you should use them for their maximum benefit.

The continual application of the plan, do, study and act cycle helps us gain knowledge and allows forgiveness in learning. It gives us the ability to apply critical thinking and devise new creative solutions to problems we face so we can learn more about things we are trying to understand.

In today's world enormous amounts of information are immediately available. But information is not knowledge. A dictionary is filled with information but it doesn't have any knowledge. Knowledge comes from critical thinking, the ability to look at a situation, analyze it, ask the right questions, and use a rational thought process to reach a logical conclusion about what is going to happen in the future. Knowledge means you will be able to make predictions of how things will happen with confidence.

With my apologies in advance to all safety managers out there, there is a huge absence of the creation of knowledge when it comes to safety. There is a ton of information about safety. All you have to do is read the rules and regulations. Common sense helps us avoid accidents from obvious hazards. We're even pretty good at making predictions about accidents with one minor detail – we can't tell when they are going to happen. Consequently many managers are willing to believe accidents are the result of fate, chance or bad luck. It's a quick and easy way to explain any single event.

Bosses also want quick answers and easy resolutions when accidents happen so everyone can get back to work as fast as possible. It's no wonder why they are task or single event oriented. It allows them to come up with the quick and plausible answer for why an accident happened. When explaining what could be done to prevent accidents their favorite, most often used words are, *if only*. *If only* the employee would have done what he was told, the accident wouldn't have happened. They never get around to thinking that *if only* the system was designed and managed better a lot more accidents could be prevented. It's not because they don't want to it's due to the fact the management system won't let them.

How do people learn? We know that in certain circumstances people can learn and solve problems much better when they work as a team than an individual. This is especially true when solving problems about work systems. But it is difficult if not impossible to take advantage of teams in the world of command and control management. Most managers believe problem solving is best done by managers with little or no help from the workers.

We perpetuate this thinking in our educational system where students are graded based on their individual abilities, not how well they work on a team. We encourage scarcity of excellence by grading on a curve so only a small amount of people can excel. There is little or no way for students to work together and help each other learn how to learn. (If they do work together we refer to it as cheating.) Ask a room full of teachers who learns more when they teach a class, the students or the teacher? Invariably their answer is, the teacher. When it comes to mastering the actual learning process let's face it, we are all pretty much on our own.

Many educators are well aware of much better ways to help people learn than the traditional methods. In the first four years of our lives we are learning machines. We learn how to talk, walk and solve problems. But the first day of school all of the creative processes are put on hold by an educational system that promotes non-critical thinking and encourages factual answers to teacher's questions. This isn't the teachers fault; it's more about the system.

Managers must understand people learn in many different ways. Some of us learn better by reading, others by attending a lecture, others by sitting in front of a computer and others by watching a video. Eventually you find out if people have learned something when it comes time to use what was taught. If you don't do something with what you've learned it doesn't matter much. And if the educational system has not helped you learn how to learn you are going to have a tough time in the new economy. You will also have great difficulty when it comes to solving safety problems created by the faults of your work system. Faults that are buried deep in the system yet impact safety every day.

We conduct most safety training as though one size fits all. The fact is we never know; how much do employees understand it? how long will they retain it?, and, will they use it? So our training effort often ends up adding more variation to safety in the work system.

Mangers must learn how pedagogy can be used to address variation of safety knowledge if they are to improve how people obtain, retain and use it at work. This is an excellent example how two parts of profound knowledge, knowledge and variation, interact with each other to contribute to reducing or increasing accidents in the system.

Psychology

Flow is the way people describe their state of mind when consciousness is harmoniously ordered, and they want to pursue whatever they are doing for its own sake. There are few things as entropic as unskilled work done under compulsion." Mihaly Csikszentmihalyi , From *Flow: The Psychology of Optimal Experience*

Psychology helps us understand people and how they relate with each other. This includes managers, hourly workers, suppliers and customers. We are all different from each other. We think differently and respond differently. (There's that variation again.) A manager must be aware of these differences and use them to optimize the effectiveness of everyone in the organization. Mr. Csikszentmihalyi describes flow as "being completely involved in an activity for its own sake. The ego falls away. Time flies. Every action, movement, and thought follows inevitably from the previous one, like playing jazz. Your whole being is involved, and you're using your skills to the utmost."

His extensive research shows you do not have to be a Buddhist monk sitting on a mountain top to achieve *flow*. One of his most interesting examples is a gentlemen living and working as a welder in a plant on Chicago's south side. He achieved flow by mastering every job in the plant and learning how to fix any machine that broke down.

Psychology impacts safety management, just like it impacts all other management activities. Unfortunately, safety management has been using B.F. Skinner's outmoded theory of behaviorism to guide how it has applied psychology for understanding relationships between people. Safety management needs to discover how to achieve flow when managing safety instead of behaviorism to change people's actions. This can be done by becoming more oriented toward achievement.

Achievement orientation

To achieve flow, psychologists have found people have an achievement orientation. Basically, this involves five interrelated ideas people use to work toward a desired end result. The elements of achievement orientation are:

1. High standards of excellence
2. Cause and effect thinking
3. The individual can and does makes a difference
4. Self-set goals
5. Feedback

The first idea, high standards of excellence, says the higher level of achievement in a person's thinking the more likely they will be focused on a standard of excellence. These are people who look at the world and seek to achieve the highest level of performance possible. (This should not be mistaken for a competitive approach to problems where a person is trying to beat someone just for the sake of winning.)

Quality and safety are terms that embody excellence. To be competitive and sustain success, companies need to make products or provide services that customers will brag about to others. Excellence is applicable to any endeavor and should be paramount in any safety effort. Excellence for safety is to make work systems safe for employees so they can do their jobs everyday without fear of being injured.

The second idea as it relates to safety is to establish the belief in the proper context of cause and effect relationships. This means we combine cause and effect with systems thinking. Many people have a tendency to believe that when it comes to accidents, fate, chance, luck, hope and magic are the primary reasons they do or do not occur. The idea things are caused and an effect comes about as a result, helps us study and learn more accurately why things happen as they do. We need to teach this on a wider scale so we avoid rather fuzzy thinking being used to solve problems. This will stop us from coming up with frivolous solutions to serious problems.

Single event thinking, assumes there is a direct connection between cause and effect which leads people to believing it is proper to search for a root cause. The theory is if you can find the one prime mover of the accident and remove it the accident won't happen again. There are all kinds of problems with this thinking. Not the least of which is, most accidents are a result of multiple interacting factors that occur randomly in the system. This is the fallacy of root cause.

Preventing accidents requires understanding the deeper nature of cause and effect relationships. This means we must take a more intense look at the system. Doing so will help us see how things interrelate and interact and how outcomes are a result of faults of these interactions. To do this we must remember cause and effect are not always closely related in time and space, a single cause can have multiple effects and some effects are the result of a combination of multiple causes that must come together just right to make the effect happen.

The elements of systems can have relationships and connections which may not be linear or visible. Cause and effect can act like an insidious disease. Psychological effects are definitely things that can have an impact long after the initial cause occurred. Something can happen to you today that may not affect you until a much later time. That's why it is difficult to find the systemic connections between cause and effect.

Management often reprimands a person who has been involved in a serious accident because they see a close connection between cause and effect. Just imagine this situation. After he recuperates a person comes back to work and his supervisor meets with him to give him hell because his finger was amputated in a punch press accident. The supervisor says something to the effect, "Well are you going to do that again?" and the employee says "Hell no, I can't really ever do it again, the finger is missing."

People like to believe they have found a simple easy explanation of why the employee did such a foolish thing. The employee didn't follow the rules so reprimand him for his mistake and move on. It shows a lack of understanding cause and effect and how it works in systems thinking. If anything, it is management planning how to react to the next accident, not planning to prevent it.

The third area of achievement is to realize an individual's effort can and does make a difference. It's a fact there are some things in life you just can't control. If you wake up and it's raining there's just not much you can do about it. In the world of work created by Taylor/Heinrich, control is taken away from the worker and put it in the hands of management. Their management system eliminated the importance of the worker in the scheme of how a system is managed. Workers just do not control a lot of what goes on in this system. Yet managers in this system conveniently hold the workers responsible for most accidents.

Neo-Taylorism perpetuates the dehumanizing of work when it creates new phrases for workers and refers to them as "human capital management." Until the 1970's Human Resources was called the Personnel department. At least back then the department had the word "person" in it.

We've taken the individual out of the system to the point where people don't see or believe their effort really does matter. Then when something goes wrong management conveniently pushes responsibility back on the individual. Perhaps one of the reasons for high turnover and absenteeism in companies is hourly people don't believe their being at work is really that important to the company. They certainly aren't treated as important assets as evidenced by the fast jettisoning of workers during economic downturns or the persistent number of employee injuries and deaths every year in the U.S.

The Taylor/Heinrich management system resulted in managers believing people who do manual labor are interchangeable and expendable. What individual workers think about how work is planned and carried out is removed from the equation. Though it is changing the attitude of white collar think and blue collar do is still prevalent.

In today's economy driven by the non-cost principle everyone's effort definitely matters. If management does a poor job of eliminating waste and making sure the number of employees matches up with the amount of work to be done a company can quickly be placed in a crisis mode. A company in crisis starts to cut corners to control costs instead of remaining calm and consistent. At this point safety is not always treated as a top priority.

In command and control managers delegate their responsibility for safety directly to the workers. They have a tendency to forget how important their effort is when designing and improving the work processes so employees will be safe. Achievement orientation restores the importance of the effort of all individuals in the work system. It creates joint participation and ownership thereby closing the loop between leading and managing when it comes to safety.

The fourth area is a strong belief in the fact that people should be setting personal goals. If a work situation is not safe, a person who has set their own standards of safety is going to think about the hazards they are creating or facing and then do something about it. I have never seen an individual set low safety standards for themselves or others at work. I have seen managers in the command and control model ignore the safety of others by not stressing safety and walking the talk on a daily basis. By encouraging self-set goals for safety the odds are good management and hourly employees are going to demand their jobs be operationally safe.

Self-set goals create an internal discipline to be safe all the time. This is the same form of discipline management depends on to run a quality management system. When intrinsic motivation is working you can trust that people will watch out for safety problems and correct them immediately.

When people are allowed to set their own safety goals they will commit to them. This means management will not have to rely on extrinsic motivators to get people to work safely. Intrinsic motivation is the key driver of self-discipline and it flourishes when people are allowed to set their own goals.

For example, in a task oriented culture management will often set a goal of reducing the accident somewhere between 5 or 10%. The reason for such low expectation is this goal may be in their performance appraisal. Over the years managers have learned how hard it is to legitimately reduce this number. But they are really settling for things to be "good enough" which is called *satisficing*.

Solutions for safety should maximize the value of the outcome which requires the optimal solution. To find out what is happening relative to safety on the job I suggest management ask employees how many accidents they want to experience at work. Of course all of them respond by saying "0" which is the maximum safety performance. Then ask them to answer the same question considering the hazards they face on their job and the number may change. Obtaining the answer to the second question provides valuable safety information. This is a much more effective method to discover safety problems than conducting safety inspections.

When employees tell you they may have one or more accidents they're saying the system they work in has some safety issues. You can put this information to good use. Just have people show you what they believe may cause them to have an accident and take action to prevent it. This type of feedback loop should be going on every day. It is truly getting the Voice of the Safety Customer into the Voice of the System.

The fifth idea is feedback. Psychologists have learned the higher the level of achievement the more people want to know about the impact of their effort. They're not looking for monetary rewards and we're not talking about positive feedback advocated by behaviorist theory.

People like to know if their effort has made a difference. Employees like to work on and fix the system. Information about accident statistics and the costs of accidents can and should be shared with workers. It allows them to see how their efforts count. (Note: This is different than what Taylor/Heinrich would do. Their idea of feedback was to evaluate the workers to let them know whether or not they have met the expectations of management or even worse, to use rewards as the feedback mechanism. It's been shown time after time this approach destroys intrinsic motivation.)

Just as some companies have found opening the books to employees is a good thing, informing employees about accidents is just as important. Publishing accident data should be done to inform and educate everyone how their efforts to improve safety counts. Accident data is an important way to allow the system to talk to you.

Achievement orientation – there is no substitute.

A new safety management theory – 14 Points for Safety Leadership

Deming's 14 points are the basis of the theory of management for continual improvement. I've taken the liberty of adapting them to focus on safety management so we have a new theory to work with for continual renewal and improvement of system/safety performance. They are not a recipe. You should not treat them as a to do list. They are more a set of values that will guide management and hourly employees when managing safety. They represent a way of learning, a philosophy you can use to make safety performance better. They are the basis of a new safety management paradigm.

1. *Create a constancy of purpose for continual improvement of safety in all company operations.*
2. *Adopt the new management philosophy for safety.*
3. *Cease dependence on mass safety inspections or any after-the-fact activity to accomplish safety.*
4. *Find problems by listening to the Voice of the Customer for safety.*
5. *Learn how to manage and employ teams for decision-making (consensus) and problem-solving of systemic safety problems.*
6. *Provide leadership instead of managership of safety.*
7. *Respond. When safety problems are exposed take action.*
8. *Eliminate the use of any type of fear to motivate people to work safely.*
9. *Break down barriers between departments that prevent good safety management.*
10. *Allow employees and work units to set their own safety goals.*
11. *Eliminate the use of safety slogans, posters, cheerleading and goals set by management for the work force.*
12. *Instill pride and joy in work when it comes to eliminating accidents.*
13. *Institute a vigorous program of educating and retraining everyone on how to apply profound knowledge and critical thinking to safety problems.*
14. *Create a culture throughout your organization that will push on the above 13 points every day.*

Elaboration of the 14 Points

1.   *Create a constancy of purpose for continual improvement of safety in all company operations.*

Management typically employs short term solutions to safety problems. Safety problems are linked with the problems of production. It is easy to get bogged down in the daily safety issues. Safety management and staff become very good at taking care of them. To handle them they implement firefighting or workaround routines. Firefighting keeps people very busy consequently little or nothing is done in the way of problem solving or system improvement. People never learn how to fix system problems they just get better at firefighting.

Attention to safety becomes a hot or cold proposition. If a safety problem is not readily apparent no attention is afforded to safety.
Management must create a culture in which safety is important every day. Not just when the obvious safety issues are recognized.

Safety, like all management, should answer two questions: What are we doing? Why are we doing it? Taking care of safety problems of the future is where the importance of constancy of purpose must be applied. Top management is responsible to all employees in this effort. Everyone should work on reducing waste and accidents to improve the competitive position of the company on a daily basis. A plan must be made to work on those things in the present and the future so safety is improved over time.

Management has obligations to do things today that will impact safety in the future. They include:

•   Analyze changes in production that will create safety issues for people that will do the work.
•   New materials may be used and must be reviewed for their impact on safety to workers.
•   Ensure effective safety training and retraining is done.
•   Costs of safety must be examined.

- How will workers jobs be made safe, i.e. free from harm when doing their existing and new jobs?
- How will safety be stressed every day?
- How will management be proactive about safety every day?
- How will we know if workers are satisfied with safety of their jobs?
- How will management put resources into safety?
- How will management train people to be problem solvers of system safety problems?

If management does not have a constancy of purpose when it comes to safety they could end up doing the opposite of everything suggested above. Not a pretty picture.

2. *Adopt the new management philosophy for safety.*

We are in a new economy. Profit is determined by how well you reduce your costs. You must keep removing all forms of waste in your operations to remain competitive. Accidents are the worst form of waste. No person is paid enough to incur an injury while doing their job.

Every single accident results in loss of money and respect of management. We can no longer live with commonly accepted levels of employee injuries, delays in safety training, poor delivery and understanding of safety education and training, mistakes and defective or improper equipment and error inducing systems.

Management at all levels must constantly work to improve safety of the work system for employees. They can only do this with the help of the employees. (Knowledge – how will it be gained?) In the new philosophy "good enough" doesn't exist and no problem means there is a problem. Everyone in the company must learn and practice this philosophy.

In this world meeting safety specifications is not good enough. We must manage all systems and processes to work together and produce results that reduce variation and interact with each other in only positive and constructive ways. We must start with a continual improvement management system.

If you don't adopt a new philosophy about how to manage safety how will you achieve continual improvement? All the companies that are leaders in their fields adopt and adapt all the time. Safety is no exception to this reality.

3 *Cease dependence on mass safety inspections or any after-the-fact activity to accomplish safety.*

Depending on frequent safety inspections is the same as planning for accidents. Traditional safety management cannot prevent all accidents. No system can. We try to inspect safety into the system. This can never work. Safety inspections are too late, ineffective and very costly. They do not improve safety anymore than giving a student a test makes them smarter or dumber. This doesn't mean there won't be any safety inspections. It means safety inspections should be conducted in upstream operations with a method to fix the system when safety issues are discovered.

Safety comes from designing and improving the production process, not from inspecting or auditing it. Inspections, accident investigations and reprimands of workers who have accidents are not corrective actions but reactive in nature. You cannot inspect more safety into your operations. A process cannot exceed the safety performance for which it was designed and then managed. Ultimately, safety must be built into processes to eliminate the need for firefighting routines that do not change or improve the system.

Conducting and collating mass safety inspections takes a lot of time and cost a lot of money. Both are better spent on more important activities. Many times they are conducted and the results are worse than doing nothing.

For example one company I worked with conducted safety inspections on a dust collection system for over five years. The employees had to keep a door open to allow for makeup air to enter the room or they could not breathe. The team we formed examined inspection sheets for the previous six months and found that even though the problem persisted it was no longer even noted on the safety inspection sheet.

At first the inefficiency of the system was noted on the safety inspections but nothing was ever done to learn why the system wasn't functioning. The team found out the exhaust system would get clogged and was difficult to clean. Maintenance missed the cleaning schedule years before and decided it was too much work to clean it. The safety inspections continued and eventually they stopped recording the problem out of frustration since nothing was ever done about it. They would just "pencil whip" the inspection. When the safety team defined the problem the Plant Manager budgeted $10,000 to clean the duct work so it would work properly. Talk about common causes! (You can't make this stuff up.)

You should replace mass safety inspections with doing work on your systems to ensure safety management controls the system from the moment an employee starts with your company until the day they leave it.

4. *Find problems by listening to the Voice of the Customer for safety.*

You need to go out and find safety problems in your operations before they cause accidents. Management should never wait around for safety problems to manifest themselves in the form of accident reports. It is management's job to work continually on the safety of the work system.

Safety management must become "customer focused" and the workers are its primary customer. Safety on-the-job is subject to the same variation and deterioration of any work process so safety problems will always exist. Develop feedback loops from workers so they can inform management about safety problems and take action to eliminate them. (See Achievement Orientation)

In business when you are truly customer focused you don't wait until something goes wrong with your product and then try to fix it. You must know your customers wants and anticipate their needs. Then do everything you can to take care of them. This is how you build "delight factors" for customers. No less an effort should be taken for safety customers. We must learn to identify "common" or "special" causes that impact safety so we can react properly. Just imagine what kind of company you would have if employees were delighted to come to work because they know management truly cares about them.

You must also be aware of the fact that customers can tell you what they expect but they don't know what they need. A need is a problem your customer has for which they do not have a solution. The solution may or may not exist. Customers didn't ask for electric light bulbs, VCR's, compact discs or I-Pods. Smart business people stay close to their customers, determine things they need and then develop products to fill that need.

This same approach should be applied to safety. Employees know about the typical safety solutions such as machine guarding, training, ergonomic design. We expect these to be taken care of when it comes to safety. I remember upon first hearing the terms Human Factors Engineering and Ergonomics in the early 1970's and thinking to myself, this will have very little acceptance in business. Today you would be hard-pressed to find a company that doesn't understand ergonomics. Ergonomics has satisfied a need and is now viewed as something expected. What are the other needs your employees have when it comes to safety?

5. *Learn how to train, manage and employ teams for consensus, decision-making and problem-solving of systemic safety problems.*

Systems, even simple systems are often too complex for one person to understand. It will take people working as a team to solve these system safety problems. Managing teams is different than the command and control management of individuals.

Management must provide people the opportunity to learn how to work and participate on teams and remove barriers to them. People need to practice to become effective team members.

Hierarchy as a form of getting things done prevents effective teamwork. People need to learn how to work on teams and must be given authority to solve safety problems. Teams will make the difference when it comes to improving safety. They are needed on a daily basis to constantly improve the system. Systems have things go wrong every day. It's like the dust on living room furniture. One person can clean it off but it will always come back. It will take a team to figure out where the dust is coming from.

6. *Provide leadership instead of managership of safety.*

You manage things and lead people. The aim of leadership is to remove the causes of failures. The responsibility of supervision must be changed from managing safety by the numbers to being leaders, facilitators, coaches and counselors of work systems.

Supervisors have been used at traffic cops when it comes to safety. They've been taught to review every single accident then talk to the worker involved to help them understand what they did wrong. This is the wrong approach. Management has a new job. It is to remove the barriers around the workers that prevent them from being able to do their jobs safely and to improve safety in work systems.

It's been said that managers do things right and leaders do the right thing. Supervisors must become system thinkers and learn how to fix the system instead of fixing the blame. They will have to acquire profound knowledge to do this.

7   *Respond. When safety problems are exposed take appropriate action.*

Ideally this should take place in the design stage. Management must create a system that will respond appropriately and immediately to data and/or information from supervisors and employees on safety problems. Feedback from workers is faster, more accurate and more important than waiting for inaccurate and less than complete safety inspections and audits.

People must learn how and when to use the **Plan, Do, Study and Act Cycle** to study and restructure the work system. (You won't need to do a PDSA to change a light bulb.) Management needs to respond and work on chronic problems such as; poor work design, superficial training, persistent and consistent accident frequencies, improper maintenance, faulty equipment and unclear operational definitions of safe work procedures.

Did an accident stem from a common or a special cause? The proper response is critical and dependent on what type of cause was responsible. The type of action you need to take for a special cause is quite different than what needs to be done to reduce variation and faults of the system itself.

    8. *Eliminate the use of any type of fear to motivate people to work safely.*

People need to be secure about management's commitment to work and be100% safe. We need to drive out fear so everyone can work effectively and safely for the company. Eliminate the use of reprimands and incentives (bribes) as management tools to control the action of employees. Fear destroys the intrinsic motivation everyone has to do a good job and to work safely. Replace management through fear with management with confidence. Never think of workers as subordinates. Do not try to motivate people by using threats of layoffs or loss of pay because of poor safety performance.

Fear comes in many forms. Feedback from people often expresses their inner fears.

- I can't tell my supervisor about my safety issue. He'll just think I'm complaining, making trouble and you don't want to be labeled as a trouble maker around here.
- Even though I know I should be working to prevent accidents in the long run, my superiors don't want that. I can't take that type of action. I don't want to lose my job. (Supervisor)
- We have to take action, like giving people time off if they have an accident. Otherwise upper management and workers won't believe we're serious about safety. (So much misunderstanding in so few words.)

- I'm not sure why we do things like reprimand people when they have an accident but there's no way I'm going to ask management for an explanation.
- I can get the safety issue fixed later. I have to make parts first.

One of the worst losses from fear is the inability of managers to best serve safety interests of workers. Supervisors are forced to make a choice between production and safety. A culture of fear will result in the manager selecting production every time unless there is a blatantly obvious life-threatening issue and even then it's a fifty-fifty proposition.

If a worker is injured, supervisors react immediately. They look for what the employee did wrong and then reprimand him. They don't look deeply into why the employee did something wrong because they may find out that management didn't do something right. This is also a form of fear.

You cannot scare people into working safely. What goes along with people being scared is anxiety and fear. A person who is afraid does not react well in stressful situation. They can panic or freeze up. This will hinder their ability to be confident and in control to ensure they will work safely. Replace fear with ability of your company to obtain and spread knowledge. Knowledge about what are the real causes of accidents. Knowledge about what must be done to fix systems so they can function without injuring people who work in them.

9. Break down barriers between departments that prevent good safety management.

All departments must learn to cooperate with each other so they can work together on solving common and special causes of accidents. Using operational definitions of what is "safe" will eliminate barriers between departments, suppliers and customers of safety. Eliminate all activities that prevent people from contributing to improving the organization. Cooperation is not a zero sum game in which one department wins and the other loses.

There are situations when one department must sacrifice to aid another so everyone wins. Doing a job safely may be perceived to take more time but in the long run it saves time if accidents are prevented. If a hazard exists, chances are taken and a worker might be injured. Faster becomes slower. The safety department must have the workers in training classes to teach them about safety. This takes them away from production. Their supervisors complain the employees aren't making parts. In the long run if the workers work safely they will be more efficient. More parts will be made with less down time for injuries. Waste is eliminated and profits go up. Morale and respect for management goes up.

One of the biggest barriers is getting the time needed to train, retrain and have hourly employees solve safety problems. There must be a system set up so workers have time to spend to evaluate and problem solve safety issues they discover daily on the job. They must also be included in pre-assessment of equipment changes to analyze how they will impact safety of the worker. All of this takes time away from production. But in the long run the company will gain. To make these scenarios reality requires cooperation between all departments.

10. Allow employees and work units to set their own safety goals.

Eliminate management set objectives for safety which are put forth in numerical quotas, incentive programs, posters, and safety slogans, none of which improve safety or the system. When worker are asked to set their own safety goals they set them higher than management. People want their work area to be 100% safe all the time not just when inspections and safety audits are conducted. They call this *tour ready every day*. It's a matter of self-preservation.

When people set their own goals they will be more committed to them. This creates ownership of safety on the job. Management will not have to monitor safety when safety permeates the culture of an organization. When employees own the safety process it will include self-monitoring and become self-sustaining activities due to their own high standards of excellence.

11. *Eliminate the use of safety slogans, posters, cheerleading and safety goals set by management for the work force.*

If employees want to create their own posters and slogans let them. But management needn't do this. It is demeaning and degrading to the pride of the workers.

When management sets safety goals it usually ends up holding people accountable for things they cannot control. (This would be the same as someone setting a goal for me of running a four-minute mile. They may set the goal for me but a t my age I would have difficulty walking a mile no matter how long it took. It would be a great stretch goal but it ain't gonna happen.) Employees work in the system and management works on it. It is easy for management to pull a goal out of a hat and tell employees to meet it. They don't have to work in the system. There is nothing wrong with setting goals when you know the method you need to use to achieve it. (See number 10.)

When it comes to safety employees don't decide what kind and how much safety training the company provides. They don't determine the pace of production or how much money will be spent on safety for guards, maintenance, etc. They can tell you what they think they will be able to achieve relative to safety. They have a built in standard for excellence because they don't want to be injured at work. They also know first hand what is going on in their work processes that can cause injuries. Having their feedback on this issue will reveal the true picture of safety in your operations.

12. *Instill pride and joy in work when it comes to eliminating accidents.*

You do this by letting people contribute to improving the system. Then remove the barriers that prevent them from doing it. Do everything in your power to make this happen. Find out, what are their ideas for improving safety on-the-job? Train people on how to use the Plan, Do, Study and Act cycle so they can solve safety problems and communicate their safety solutions, innovations and ideas.

Poor safety devastates the morale and respect for management. Improving safety puts pride and joy back into all jobs. What will management do to make sure employee ideas are implemented, tested and improved?

Forget about annual performance appraisals which destroy the intrinsic motivation of employees to do a good job and prevents teamwork. Stop using safety incentive programs to attempt to motivate workers to be safe. These are nothing more than sophisticated schemes evolved from Taylorism and B.F. Skinner. They have no place in modern management philosophy or techniques.

13. *Institute a vigorous program of educating and retraining everyone on how to apply profound knowledge and critical thinking to safety problems.*

Everyone must learn profound knowledge, teamwork and problem solving tools. Help them apply these tools to their work. Don't have one training session every 10 years. Training is an ongoing process. People need to be trained for job skills. They also need to keep learning. It's not enough to improve your processes. Your people need to be improving as well. Not just their job skills but their ability to critically analyze situations and take action when needed. Have them apply the PDSA cycle in all of your operations at every appropriate opportunity, especially when it comes to safety.

14. *Create a culture throughout your organization that will push on the above 13 points every day.*

Culture is hard to define but it is what your workers face on a daily basis. Culture is the values, thinking, beliefs and behavior that drive your company. Culture is what you do when you don't consciously think about what you are doing. Make the 14 points real in your organization and you will create a positive constructive culture.

When you are committed to a paradigm shift you will have to work with and persuade people who have a lot invested in the existing paradigm. They can be blinded by what Joel Barker calls the "paradigm effect" which happens when a person has such a strong commitment to an outmoded paradigm they just won't see what is going on. The paradigm effect prevents people from being able to grasp or understand anything about the new one. When this happens what may be perfectly obvious to you will be totally hidden to them. There are all kinds of examples of this. Imagine buggy whip manufacturers looking at what Henry Ford was doing in the early 1900's.

I mention this because the way to see things differently about safety is to be guided by the 14 Points and learn about and obtain profound knowledge. People invested in traditional safety paradigm may not be able to see the obvious reasons for participating in the new one you are proposing. It will be up to you to help them obtain profound knowledge and apply the 14 Points of safety leadership.

The Taylor/Heinrich paradigm has been around since the 1950's and it accomplished many things for safety management. During that time we have been doing a lot of paradigm enhancement. The rules, protocols and standards were applied but in today's economy the paradigm has a lot of problems it doesn't solve, not the least of which is how to apply continual improvement philosophy to daily work routines.

Since the 1980's we've been tinkering with the safety paradigm. We've introduced some of the basic theories of psychology and called it behavior based safety with some quality theory methods thrown in. But we haven't been able to make the transformation to continual improvement. Until now we have not put forth a new safety management theory.

Part 4

CRISP: A NEW WAY OF THINKING AND MANAGING SAFETY

"Figures on accidents do nothing to reduce the frequency of accidents. The first step in the reduction of the frequency of accidents is to determine whether the cause of the accident belongs to the system or from a specific set of conditions." W. Edwards Deming

The aim of Part 4 is to examine concepts about managing safety in a new way. It's been shown that American mangers understand and generally know how to use the scientific method. They can apply it to a particular task. They don't know how to apply it to a system. We have to break away from what we have done in the past if we are going to manage safety in a new way.

Taylorism has left a legacy of companies unable to compete in today's economy. There are numerous American companies who have applied a new theory of management, experienced success but only temporarily. In most cases the people who led the culture change retired or moved on and are replaced with managers who are still Taylorized. They inevitably revert to command and control methods and destroy what progress was made towards continual improvement. Ford Motor Company is the most glaring example of this in the late 1980's and early 1990's.

If we are going to compete in the world economy we must be able to think differently about how people manage work systems. We have been doing this for quality and now we must do it for safety.

Insoluble problems

"We could teach everybody in half an hour how to do simple statistical process analysis.... We can't in a half an hour persuade people to use it."

David Langford, former teacher at Mt. Edgecomb Alaska HS who used continual improvement ideas for education in his classroom.

"To a mouse, cheese is cheese. That's why mousetraps work." Wendell Johnson

"Insanity is doing the same thing over and over and expecting different results." Albert Einstein

Traditional managers have come to believe preventing employee accidents is a problem with an easy solution. I've heard many top managers and safety directors exclaim "Safety is just a matter of getting people to use their common sense. The problem is common sense isn't so common."

This sounds good. It has a facile logic to it. Unfortunately, it doesn't begin to solve anything. Safety management presents an *insoluble* problem and that is, management doesn't know exactly what it takes to stop employee accidents. After all the years of study directed at safety management you will not find a single convergent solution offered for the answer to the question, how do you prevent employee injuries? You will find many divergent opinions.

Studies have shown when people are coping with insoluble problems they go through the following stages.

- First, they are trained to make a habitually given choice when confronted by a given problem.

  In the case of safety, managers and most of the general population, believe preventing accidents is just a matter of instructing people to use their common sense and correcting their unsafe behavior in the future. This is done over and over every day in the U.S. It's how they've been trained.

- Second, they are terribly shocked when they find the conditions have changed and the choice doesn't produce the expected results.

  We are changing from mass production to lean manufacturing but still using Taylor/Heinrich model to manage safety.

These choices for solutions don't work in lean and the new management model. We believe safety is the same for all processes even though the new processes are fundamentally different than the old ones.

- Third, whether through shock, anxiety, or frustration, they may fixate on the original choice and continue to make that choice regardless of the consequences.

Since managers don't know any other way and aren't interested in spending any time or energy learning a new one, they keep relying on traditional safety methods. The results are the same or worse.

- Fourth, they refuse to act at all.

This is done very subtly when managers spend their time prioritizing, putting other things like production and quality ahead of safety, figuring they will get around to it eventually resulting in nothing being done. Firefighting and workarounds are also ways managers don't take action on the problems that really cause accidents. Managers often spend time mistakenly working on symptoms of the safety problem which also keeps them from taking action.

- Fifth, when by external compulsion they are forced to make a choice, they again make the one they were originally trained to make – but still get the same results.

An example of this is when a company has been involved in a serious accident. At that point they face large fines imposed by OSHA. Top management responds by beating on middle managers about poor safety performance. Management's answer is to become even more focused on intensifying safety inspections, accident investigations and changing the behaviors of the workers to get them to act safe. Safety outcomes may get better for awhile but accidents eventually return, sometimes at higher levels.

- Finally, even with a solution to the problem clearly in front of them, to be attained simply by making a different choice they don't see it and experience extreme frustration.

    Management fails to understand why they should use continual improvement methods for safety. They just can't understand why traditional safety solutions don't work. They do the same thing over and over yet expect different results. [16]

You may have observed this pattern of thinking in your company. Psychologists call it *cognitive dissonance*. A person can be so committed to an idea that when presented with evidence his belief is wrong he will come away not only unable to accept the evidence for the new idea but even more committed to his idea of what is the truth than he was before.

We know that mice can't solve problems like human beings. So we can understand that when they are faced with insoluble problems created in lab experiments, they cease to care about themselves. They experience what is the equivalent of a nervous breakdown. (Or they will just go ahead and try to grab the cheese, even though it is in a mousetrap.) But humans have the ability to think and reason. We can come up with new ways of looking at problems that were thought to be insoluble and develop solutions to them. We need to apply this ability to safety.

Masaaki Imai, author of Kaizen, says there is a major difference in the way of thinking between Japanese and Western management. Kaizen takes a process-oriented view of things and Western management tends to focus on reviewing the performance of people relative to the results with no attention paid to their efforts made.

American managers spend much more time on conflict management and resolution than truly fixing the system. We do pretty much the very same thing for safety. We focus on making people behave safely instead of fixing the system. To address what are perceived to be insoluble safety problems we need a new theory. The Neo-Taylor-Heinrich paradigm will not suffice in the new work methods or what some are calling a thinking production system. It's time for a paradigm shift in safety management.

Things we need to know

For the last twenty-five years I have been learning a new way of thinking about safety and teaching it to management and hourly employees The following are some of the more important characteristics about people and organizations I've observed in that time.

1. People do not come to work to make scrap or to injure themselves.
2. All systems are broken, waiting to be fixed. They do not heal or fix themselves.
3. Generally speaking, people working on their own are not good problem solvers. It's not that people aren't smart it's just the fact that past management practices did not require or even discouraged problem solving skills. Consequently people lose interest in honing their problem solving skills. Also as we age generally people lose the spark of creativity necessary to want to solve a new problem.
4. Conversely, people can learn fairly quickly how to work as a team to solve problems.
5. The use of fear destroys the intrinsic motivation people have to do a good job and to work safely.
6. After people are trained on the basic problem solving tools they seldom use them again on their own. (Flow charts, cause and effect, pareto, etc.) They have a tendency to use them once or twice and that's it. Even though they know they work. Using these basic tools is not optional. You must push people to use them. (It's one of the burdens of being a leader.)
7. People want to contribute to the success of the company they work for.
8. If a manager is not a systems thinker they will have a tendency to blame an individual for just about everything that goes wrong in their operations. (I know this because I did this many times when I was a manager and I still see it every day.)
9. We almost never get things right the first time.
10. Middle management is the key to success when changing the system. You can get people to push from the top and from the bottom but when you really want things to happen it's the middle that counts.

Basically, if you keep these points in mind when you are trying to work on improving safety you will have a better than average chance of making a difference. The problem is in a command and control management system these characteristics are not acknowledged or denied and therefore ignored. If you are going to take advantage of them you will have to employ a different management theory.

CRISP – a new management model

The first thing you need to accomplish when changing something is to gain people's trust. I'm advocating a new safety management model which will obviously require a lot of change. It is a new system for how safety will be delivered to people in your organization. At the risk of having it perceived as a fad I call the process CRISP™ which is an acronym for **C**ontinual **R**enewal and **I**mprovement of **S**ystem/Safety **P**erformance. The CRISP model changes everything about managing safety.

There is a saying that anything not worth doing is not worth doing well. The traditional command and control approach to safety will not serve people in the new economy where continual improvement is the goal. CRISP is a new philosophy of safety management not just doing the same things better.

The diagram below depicts the new management model of CRISP. The model works from the center outward. It starts with a new theory of management which is linked to methods, leadership and outcomes. Instead of trying to maintain the status quo through rules, regulations and bureaucracy the goal of management in this model is to achieve continual improvement in all outcomes of organizational activities.

The New Management Model - CRISP™
(Continual Renewal & Improvement of System/Safety Performance)

At the center or inner circle of the model is CRISP a new management theory. The role of management in command and control theory is to Plan, Organize, Implement, Monitor and Control. Control in this world is focused on making workers do what management directs. The ultimate goal here is to maintain the status quo. Although the focus of CRISP is on continual improvement it is also concerned with control. But control in this context is directed at learning how to make the outcomes of the system satisfy the needs of all of your customers. The safety of people working in your operations is a key outcome. In this model safety is not a separate function of management as depicted on an organizational chart. Safety management must be integrated with all facets of the business. This thinking will change the culture of your organization.

The second circle shows just some of the new methods required for continual improvement of safety. The 14 Points and profound knowledge are in this ring because they will help you observe and study work processes so you can fix the system. Obtaining profound knowledge combined with the other methods will help you gain new and different insights about the world of work. Learning how and why to use them will help you focus on things that are truly important for taking care of your internal safety customers as well as the ultimate customers of your product or service. You will have to spend time listening to them and anticipating their needs. You will also learn how to use data so you can test your new theories to see if they work. These methods will replace command and control techniques such as safety inspections and accident investigations. The more you use them the more upstream preventive actions will be performed resulting in less things going wrong in the system.

The next circle involves leadership. The most important work of leaders in the transformation is to ensure barriers to implementing CRISP are removed. The three key elements of leadership in the new management model will involve teams, tools and technology. The barriers to all three are formidable. The leader's job will be to guide people and remove barriers to each of these. Leaders will have to show and teach people why teams are important and how they will be used to manage systems. The leader's job will be to mentor people to learn how to be positive, constructive team members and then create effective teams. They will also have to lead in the effort to balance technology with people's needs so they can be more efficient.

For example it will take leadership to ensure the individual's personal identity is not lost by working on a team. Leaders must ensure individuals will be given the authority to block team decisions if they have a factual disagreement with the team. Ironically, giving teams the power to reach consensus will increase the stature of the individual in the organization. This approach to managing will be counterintuitive to traditional managers with their history of not having to share any power with hourly workers. It will take time and experience for them to accept that giving up their power is a better way to control things. It will take careful leadership to achieve this transformation.

The outer circle represents the outcomes of the system; quality, productivity, safety and competitive position. Ultimately all of these will improve as a result of the new management theory, methods and leadership. The details of the acronym are as follows:

CONTINUAL means a steady repetition, over and over again. Always keep in mind Point Number 1 of the 14 Points, we must work with a constancy of purpose.

Most people use the term "continuous improvement" without thinking about what it really means. There is a subtle but important distinction between continuous vs. continual. "Continuous" means something happening without interruption. For example there is a continuous flow of water over a water fall.

The word "continual" is defined as a close prolonged recurrence, happening over and over, regularly. An example is...a blinking light.

Think about your efforts to improve quality, productivity and safety. They are continual not continuous. No company I know of works on quality, productivity or safety improvement 100% of the time. If they did that would be continuous and no work would get done.

The fact is employees need to spend most of their time doing the work required of their jobs. They spend time intermittingly on improving the quality and safety of their work which is on a continual basis. There is nothing you can do about it because work is really what you get paid for. On the other hand quality events such as improvement projects, quality circles and stopping the line happen repeatedly over time. In other words your improvement efforts are on-going versus non-stop. The results are continual improvement of quality, productivity and safety and there is nothing wrong with that.

Work is designed to be continuous but it never really turns out that way. There are always interruptions for meetings, down time due to problems, accidents, etc. We would always like to have safety designed into the process before it starts so we wouldn't have to worry about it. But even if it is, processes are subject to variation and degrade over time. That means they will always be changing and losing capabilities including the safety designed in the system. That is why we must have continual improvement of safety.

RENEWAL means the act of renewing which is to restore or re-establish on a new, usually improved, basis.

How many times have you been involved in a new quality or safety program only to see it fade away or be rejected and replaced when a new manager takes over? Often the new approach is based solely on the personality or bias of your new boss. Workers call this the flavor-of-the-month approach. People in your organization must know why it exists and be able to identify what it stands for. You have to be careful not to reject something just because it is new and different. The only way to improve things is to try something new and different. People must be given freedom to decide how to respond to what's going on around them and change things so they will get better, not deteriorate.

To manage for continual improvement requires renewal of the mental and manual labor of everyone in the company. In reality managing for continual improvement every day is hard work. It's hard for managers to allot time to work to let people work on the system and still keep up production. (I've heard this described as trying to change a flat tire on your car while you keep traveling at 30 miles per hour. Not a very easy task.) This means you are open for business during renovation and it goes on everyday.

There will always be starts and stops to improvement efforts and this is frustrating. But people thrive when they work intensely on things they enjoy. They take pride and joy in their work. To make this happen you must create a positive, constructive culture in which people can renew their efforts, ability and energy every day. It isn't enough to improve your processes. You must learn how to balance improvement efforts with production and there is no simple formula for doing this. Your people must also be renewing their individual skills and ability to think and solve problems. It is easy to do this intermittently but very difficult to make it part of your daily work routine.

IMPROVEMENT means to make things better than they were before.

No matter what your present level of quality, productivity or safety performance is, it can always be improved. This includes things you do for safety such as training, communication, learning and promotion. There is always a better way. To improve you must know how your system is doing now then strive to find ways to make things better in the future. Meeting specifications is no longer "good enough." You must work to make your processes operate with minimum variation from the target and then look for ways to improve that.

SYSTEM is defined as interdependent components working together in a cooperative manner to accomplish a purpose. SAFETY means to be free from harm when working in a system.

People must learn how to study and improve systems. What is a system? To study and understand a system you must employ *systems thinking*, which is the discipline of seeing wholes. Most people employ single event thinking with painstaking accuracy which is not that useful for understanding systems. We've been taught that to understand what goes on in a process you should separate and isolate individual pieces of the whole. When you do this you lose the ability to determine how parts of the system work together and affect each other. A system cannot achieve high productivity without high quality and high safety. You will have to learn to focus on your system to be able to see what is going on in it to make improvements. You will have to learn to see how things are connected even when it is not obvious.

Systems thinking and safety go hand in hand. A system must be made safe or it will cause harm to the people who work in it or around it. All systems will produce accidents. To keep accidents at an absolute minimum you must work on the system all the time. Work systems do not improve by themselves. They will always susceptible to variation and that means things can go wrong. A system that is not safe cannot accomplish its intended purpose. There will be accidents, waste, scrap and rework. There will also be the hidden impact of poor safety in the form of lack of respect for management, low morale and a negative culture. To counteract this you should work to have a self correcting system with processes that restore order through freedom.

PERFORMANCE means what is accomplished by both outputs and people in the system.

Performance is important because it provides feedback about your efforts to improve your systems. Data is important but you must understand that some things in a system cannot be measured. Safety like quality is an output of both the work system and the management system.

There are hard and soft attributes in all systems. It is not difficult to measure the hard data like the output of a manufacturing system and it is wise to do so. But how do you measure things like; trust, pride and joy in work, the hidden costs of accidents or an unhappy customer? These are also very important but extremely difficult to quantify. You must learn how to listen to both the hard and soft outcomes of your system so you can improve it.

In the new management model people will think differently about safety in the following ways:

1. Safety will be customer focused. Employees are the first and foremost customers of safety management and their families are the next most important.

2. Management must work constantly go get the Voice of The Safety Customers into the Voice of The Process. Safety should not apply the law of diminishing returns to calculate costs of safety improvement projects.

3. Safety and quality will be the umbrella over all operations in the company. Everyone will understand what "safe" means because it will be defined using "operational definitions." Safe will have the same meaning to everyone in the organization everyday.

4. Improving safety will be considered a strong competitive strategy. It increases productivity, morale and supplier relationships.

5. All-employees, all departments will be involved in improving safety everyday. Heavy reliance will be placed on the intrinsic motivation all people have to work safely.

6. When it comes to safety, prevention is better than the cure. Upstream actions are sought and taken to create built-in safety. Working upstream means to anticipate safety customer's needs before they are aware of them.

7. Teams will be used to manage and solve safety problems. They will be trained to use a structured, disciplined, graphical approach to defining safety problems and then come up with creative and elegant solutions. Their solutions will be focused on fixing-the-system not the blame for accidents.

8. Safety will be integrated into all operational systems, especially new designs and updates.

9.   Safety improvement will depend on co-operation, not competition, between all systems, departments and people to achieve goals.

10.   Profound knowledge will be the new lens for looking at safety in the system.

A new perspective on accident causation

Most managers in the 1980's and 90's were exposed to Deming and to a greater or lesser extent tried to incorporate his thinking into their quality programs. Unfortunately, his ideas about employee safety were not widely known nor were they applied with keen insight. At first Deming's ideas are difficult to understand because he presents a philosophy, not a technique. His ideas require you to think about what's happening and eventually to change most of how you think about what you are doing now. It means you have to start from a new place.

Clare Crawford-Mason, who worked with Deming for many years, says she believes American managers have difficulty adopting Deming's ideas because his way is hard and they want things to be easy. She say's they want "instant pudding." CRISP is not going to be instant pudding and if it were easy everyone would be doing it now.

What Deming said about safety challenges the basic foundations of the Taylor/Heinrich model. In his book, Out of the Crisis, p. 478, he describes five principles for Improvement for Living. His fifth one states:

"No system whatever be the effort put into it, be it manufacturing, maintenance, operation, or service will be free of accidents."

This statement contradicts a basic edict of traditional safety management which says <u>all accidents</u> can be prevented. In other words you should be able to run an operation accident free 100% of the time. It's a nice theory unfortunately it has never been done. In the world of mere mortals no system or process can ever be perfect. (See Safety Myth No. 2)

What does cause accidents?

Managers who adhere to traditional safety theory employ single event thinking. That is why it is standard operating procedure to complete a full blown investigation after every single accident. Investigators are trained to examine what was happening at the moment just prior to the accident. For them cause and effect are closely linked in time and space. They have been taught the formula below:

Unsafe Acts + Unsafe Conditions + Time = an accident

Heinrich's theory suggests that unsafe acts are 88% of the reason for accidents and unsafe conditions account for the remaining 12%. The formula makes it simple and easy to understand why accidents happen. Unfortunately it's simplicity on the near side of complexity. Unsafe acts and conditions are fairly easy to visualize and discern. The basic flaw in this line of thinking is the fact that unsafe acts and conditions are not causes but symptoms of things gone wrong in the management system. And the management system is filled with complexity.

The formula provides a superficial explanation of why accidents happen. It assumes everything up to the point in time just before the accident happened worked properly and the causes of the accident are the actions that occurred just a few seconds prior to what went wrong. This assumption prevents people from connecting things that happened before that and may have actually had a role in causing the accident. These include things like poor safety training, bad purchasing decisions about safety equipment, the pressure to increase production at any given moment, etc. At best these are given cursory attention; at worst they are totally ignored. They are not always closely linked in time and space yet they can and do have effects that cause accidents. These are the web of all of the elements in the system hence the interconnectedness and interactions are linked together and these are the common causes.

Every operation has hazards that can cause harm to people working around them. The company has a duty and responsibility to hire and train people how to do a job properly. The training should be sufficient in its scope to show workers what is expected of them and how to do every job safely. But little attention or thought is given to how effective safety training is over time. It is highly unusual or non-existent for safety training to be linked to consideration of production. For example workers should be trained that it is OK to stop working and notify management if safety issues arise. This would require management and workers have full working knowledge about operational definitions and most do not possess this knowledge.

So if an employee is doing something deemed unsafe the management system has failed in its basic obligation of protecting the worker from exposure to hazards. Of course this does not address those instances where an employee acts improperly and defies all logic which are the special causes Deming describes and happen only about 1% of the time.

Common and special causes of accidents

Deming helps us gain a better understanding and take us to a higher level of understanding about what causes accidents when he says:

"To look for something special, and to take action on a particular man, or on the particular piece of apparatus that went wrong, or on an installation, when the cause of the accident is a common cause that could have lead to the accident at the hands of other men, or with other pieces of apparatus, or with other installations, is doomed to failure. Accidents that arise from common causes will continue to happen with their expected frequency and variation until the system is correct. The split is possibly 99 per cent from the system, and 1 per cent from carelessness. I have no figures on the split, and there will not be any figures till people understand accidents with the aid of statistical thinking."

Statistical thinking is a way of studying systems with some tools attached. The tools help you to collect, analyze and interpret data. (SPC charts, Pareto, DOE, FMEA, etc.) Deming is the first person to talk about "common causes" of accidents. He says they are responsible for as much as 99% of all accidents and only 1% of accidents are caused by the carelessness of workers. This theory is in direct conflict with traditional safety theory where 88% of accidents are believed to be caused by *unsafe acts* committed by the person just prior to or at the moment the accident happened.

Common causes are the interconnections and interactions between the essential parts of the system. Work systems comprise of people, materials, methods, machinery and equipment and environment. Each of these has variation. When the interactions of common causes take place everything does not run smoothly. The interactions of common causes can create faults that lead to accidents, scrap and defects. These are built into the system. Special causes are things that are unusual to the system. They don't normally exist.

It is important to learn to recognize what type of problem you are dealing with so you can handle it properly. Solving problems stemming from common causes differs from ones created by special causes. The two types of variation can only be discerned reliably on a control chart. That is why Deming advocates the thinking of statistical control to help us recognize the difference between the two conditions.

He explains:

"If you react to data in a non-statistical fashion and treat common cause variation as local faults, one of several bad consequences will occur. The best of the evils is that people will ignore you, and may learn not to respect you. The employees may, however, do something unnatural or non-repeatable to "oil this week's squeaking wheel." This "knee-jerk" response is also confusing, demoralizing, and increases variability in the long term (over control). In any case, the creative spirit and energy of the employees are depleted. Then no long-term improvements are likely to occur."

All of us have made the mistake of reacting to an accident as though it was the result of a special cause, something a person did that was unusual in an operation, when in fact it was due common causes, problems in the system. Until I was introduced to Deming I treated all accidents as though the employee had done something wrong. That's how I was trained to react. The consequences were exactly what he said they would be.

Things can get even more confusing when common causes are manifested later as special causes. For example when an employee is caught not wearing personal protective equipment the basic assumption by management is the person messed up. They have been caught performing an unsafe action and are violating a perfectly reasonable and legitimate safety rule. It is assumed the employee is the cause and can control his actions. No thought is given about whether or not the system failed the employee which could happen in many ways or to design the system so PPE would not be necessary.

Understanding common and special causes requires brutal honesty by everyone. If someone has been told to wear personal protective equipment (PPE) and they don't most people believe it is reasonable to hold them responsible. Workers are supposed to follow the safety rules. We don't consider the existence of faults of common causes in the system that may influence whether or not employees wear PPE. For example the PPE might be too small, too tight, very uncomfortable and dirty, damaged or not available. I have witnessed all of these situations over the years. On more than one occasion I've seen respirators with mold growing in them yet management expected employees to wear them. These examples are the result of a number of minor common causes that are manifested as what one could mistake for a special cause.

Intuitively you know there are some kinds of connections between the problems noted above but you can't connect the dots with the deterministic approach advocated in command and control. It's the same as the comparing Newtonian physics with quantum mechanics where cause and effect have quite a different relationship. In the former it is believed that to understand what is happening the parts of the whole are separated and studied to determine which one is causing things to go wrong. It is assumed everything can be figured out following this method. The world is mechanistic and machine like where cause and effect are closely connected in time and space. In the latter there is a realization that even though things are separated in space and time, like sub-atomic particles they are still connected and influence each other. The quantum world challenges what we know about relationships, connectedness, prediction and control.

So we can start to understand that cause and effect can act differently than what Newtonian thinking has taught us. Common causes can have effects at great distances in time and space.

Special causes are situations that don't normally exist in the system. They come and go without warning. They are not planned. It's unlikely they will be repeated so you must look for them immediately or you may never find the cause. Information about special causes may also dissipate very quickly. Traditional safety management advocates investigating every single accident as though something unusual happened. This means you are probably treating most employee accidents as though they are a result of a special cause when it is more likely they stem from faults in the system that have built up over time.

When a person does something wrong we assume they do it of their own free will. For instance an employee ignores a safety rule. We conclude corrective action is a simple matter of instructing the employee and reinforcing the need for them to comply with the rule in the future. How else could you see it? What's wrong with pointing out a person's mistake and expecting them to learn from the feedback?

There is often more to a situation than meets the eye. When an employee forgets to wear PPE or fails to work safely management assumes the employee is 100% at fault and must be held accountable. Management can see no reason to look for something else that could be wrong in the system. But the important question to ask is, why didn't the system produce the outcome we desire? Are there faults in our safety management system? We have spent a lot of time and energy training managers about the techniques of how to investigate the actions of the workers. The problem is; most managers don't have a clue about how to investigate or examine the system. The reason; they are not *system thinkers*.

How do we find out what allowed the safety problem to exist? Looking for the faults in the system takes a lot of hard work, time and self-criticism. It is much easier to just remind the employee that next time just do what they have been told and ignore or not worry about faults in the system. (I've heard this referred to as common cause stupidity.) This approach creates the habit of treating most problems as people problems (special causes) so we never get around to fixing the system. It is easier to firefight. It is also the beginning of no long term improvement Deming describes in his quote above.

The fact is, to be effective you need to learn how to discern and react to common and special causes. If you are dealing with a common cause, which is 85-99% of the time, you start by looking at the system and strive to understand how things worked to allow miscues and accidents to occur. Armed with profound knowledge you know that systems, even simple ones, are too complex for any one person to understand. You are aware common causes are best studied by a team of people familiar who possess profound knowledge. They will apply a structured, disciplined approach to define and analyze the system that can lead to creative, innovative and elegant solutions to the problem. That's what the Plan Do Study and Act cycle is all about.

If in fact you are dealing with a special cause and you recognize it, the local manager and/or worker can handle it. Special causes do not require a change in the system. People do have control over them and can take corrective action on their own. For example, if an employee accidently drops a soda bottle and broken glass is all over the floor. This is something the employee can take care of by themselves. It's appropriate to treat this as a special cause.

The following is another real life example of how common and special causes can be misconstrued. Every week a supervisor provides protective gloves to employees. To control costs he decided employees required no more than three pairs of gloves per week. (This was just an arbitrary number based on no research or data.) Some employees wear out the gloves faster than others or some may lose a pair. They may need four or five pair in a week. It doesn't matter. The supervisor would only give them their allotment of three pair. If they need more than three they are out of luck. He felt he had to teach the workers a lesson. He was holding them accountable. They had to work without the gloves until the new week started; an example of "over control" if there ever was one. Are you dealing with common or special causes? Or both? How you react to and solve this problem is critical. In this case we let the hourly people hand out the gloves. The perceived abuse stopped.

Treating an accident or problem as though it is a result of a special cause when it originates from a common cause does nothing to change or fix the system. It is a knee-jerk reaction in the search for a quick and simple solution. If you are lucky and you are working on a special cause you may do some good. But if you react as though the employee did something wrong when it was a failure in your system you are just going to make matters worse. You won't know you've done something wrong. But the workers will.

Of course the target for safety is always zero injuries. But even in the best systems there will always be variation so you can't hit your target every time. Nonetheless your actions should always be directed at moving the mean number of accidents consistently closer to zero. And here's the rub. Common causes, which prevent you from doing this, are buried deep in your system. They are difficult to discover, study, understand and change. Like they say if this was easy anyone could do it.

Studying the system brings you closer to the truth about why accidents occur. But there is another big challenge when studying the system and that is complexity. Some accidents may be a result of multiple common causes occurring non-sequentially. One person cannot possibly know everything about a system. And you'll find when you push the system, it pushes back. It will not give up the answers easily. You will learn, as Peter Senge has pointed out, cause and effect are not always closely related in time and space.

Non-systems thinkers, which include most traditional managers, have a very difficult time accepting this. It doesn't make sense in their command and control world. Their ultimate goal is to control workers so safety can meet specifications spelled out in rules and regulations. They want simple, easy and quick results.

Continual improvement requires the use systems thinking, the discipline of seeing wholes. If you are going to improve a system you have to know what kind of trouble you are in so you can act appropriately. You want to know if you are dealing with something in or outside the system. This prevents you from wasting time by treating a special cause as though it was a common cause or vice versa. The problem for people who don't use systems thinking is their inability to accept the reality that the system itself, not a person or a process in it, is to blame for most of the things that go wrong. If you are guided by single event thinking you won't be able to see this. You just won't get it.

The investigation team found the root cause of the sinking of the Titanic was the poor judgment of Captain Edward J. Smith. The blame was placed directly on him. The advice given in the final report that the accident could have been avoided by simply heeding the warning the Titanic had been given about ice flows in the area, is a vivid example of non-systems or single event thinking. It prevents people from seeing or examining what role all of the other parts in the system played in the accident.

Unfortunately we haven't come very far when it comes to applying systems thinking to understanding accidents. The Titanic tragedy occurred in 1912. The Nuclear power accident at Three Mile Island for which the investigators concluded the cause was primarily the fault of a bunch of hapless operators, took place in 1979, sixty-seven years later.

Showing that single event thinking is still the major influence of how we view accidents and a very acceptable way of examining them.

In November 2007 the initial reaction to a ship colliding with the San Francisco Bay Bridge shows we still focus first on blaming someone when an accident happens. The following was reported by the Bay City News Wire:

"With more than 40,000 gallons of oil still saturating Bay Area waters as of Sunday, a federal criminal investigation into the cause of last week's spill is under way, according to the U.S. Coast Guard.

Human error aboard a tanker ship appears to be what caused the 900-foot Cosco Busan to crash into a San Francisco-Oakland Bay Bridge tower Wednesday, gashing a hole into the ship from which approximately 58,000 gallons of oil poured into the San Francisco Bay, the Coast Guard reported.

Sen. Dianne Feinstein, D-Calif., said at a news conference Sunday that everything she has heard about the oil spill "indicates that this should not have happened."

These reactions and conclusions do not take into account the extremely heavy fog at the time of the accident. Or the fact the pilot of the vessel guiding it through the bay had concerns with the electronic devices including the radar and charting equipment. He made adjustments to it and reviewed them with the captain. The ship was recently sold and the crew and captain were new to the vessel. It you think about it, the situation had many common causes and was an accident just waiting to happen.

Examples of common causes in routine work processes

Over the years I've asked hundreds of managers what they think causes most accidents. The most frequent answer is; carelessness or people not paying attention. When managers believe this no real safety improvement can take place. They will be content to focus corrective action on individuals as the best method to reduce accidents.

Common causes are inherent in any constant cause system. They exist in all work systems and are responsible for most work accidents. Until managers understand the difference between common and special causes they will continue to conduct wild goose chases to blame and hold individual workers accountable for most accidents.

It's understandable that managers are not comfortable talking about common causes. It's because they feel they are being attacked since they design the system. They have a bias to believe the system is working properly and the unsafe actions of workers are the main reason things go wrong. Consequently their goal isn't to examine and fix the system but to fix the blame. They have to realize they are using the wrong management theory and that is why faults in the system are not being discovered and corrected.

Here are some additional real life examples of common causes of safety problems I've seen over the years:

- Employees incur lacerations when using a new type of box cutter. New ones were purchased and were of low quality. The safety latch designed to prevent people's fingers from coming in contact with the blade failed after a few uses. When this happened the guard for the blade failed and their hands slipped down on the cutting edge of the blade slicing their fingers. The original cutters had no such problem and no lacerations occurred. (Data confirmed this.)

  Upon investigation it was learned the corporate purchasing department, located in a different city and having no idea how the box cutters were used or how well they performed, was able to save $0.25 on each new cutter. The purchasing people did not take safety of the cutters into consideration. Safety was not an issue in their minds. They didn't have to use the new cutters.

  The minimal costs to the company for each laceration ranged from $50-100! The workers could not get purchasing to switch back to better quality cutters. They were told by supervision to be more careful when using the new cutters. To save a few pennies, management was losing thousands of dollars and the respect of its workers. Purchasing won, safety lost, the company lost. How much they lost will never be known.

- Another situation is played out many times at different companies. Employees point out powered industrial trucks travel at a high rate of speed in aisles where people walk when taking their breaks. Some people have even been hit by the vehicles and minor injuries are incurred. Over the years some of the injuries were serious.

The vehicles have to travel in the area to deliver parts to work stations. There is no other route for the drivers to take. When employees are hit, the drivers are reprimanded and told to pay more attention to the pedestrian traffic in the area. Drivers complain the pedestrians don't watch where they are walking.

The pedestrians are cautioned about how dangerous the plant is and it is their responsibility to watch out for the industrial trucks. Nothing is done to reroute the vehicles or smooth out the production so the drivers don't have to hurry or drive in the area when employees take breaks. Nothing is done to eliminate the use of the vehicles.

- And yet another often repeated scenario. An employee reports for work and is told they must attend mandated safety training before they handle hazardous waste. (The mandated training could be for any other safety topic, lock out, etc.) A qualified supervisor is supposed to oversee the training at all times.

After the first 15 minutes in which a video is being played the supervisor is called away to a jobsite emergency. The supervisor tells the newly hired employee to watch the remaining videos and he will return as soon as he can. The supervisor is gone for the remainder of the workday.

The same thing happens the next day but when the supervisor is called to the jobsite he takes the new employee with him and puts him to working handling hazardous waste. The employee does not complete the mandated safety training.

The employee told me about this incident three years after it happened. He never completed the mandated training yet the supervisor put documentation in his file that he had. If I hadn't inadvertently found this out, no one would have known the facts about the situation.

These are examples of faults or deficiencies of common causes built into the system, which are the primary causes of accidents, not the workers nor the managers. These causes are not close to the effects in time and space. Individually on their own they may not seem like a big deal to some people, especially those who don't have to work in these conditions. But when you have to face the potential problems they create every day they are very big and very real.

In the first example, purchasing was pressed to save a few cents without understanding the total costs of their actions. Accidents continue months, sometimes years after these types of decisions are made.

In the second, the system is designed poorly. Again accidents occurred months and years after the layout was designed.

The third is an example of the persecution of production. This is an unwritten but understood law that when a manager is forced to make a choice between production vs. safety production wins. These are common causes buried deep in the system. If you aren't aware of common causes and how the system itself impacts safety of the workers you will never find them. You won't even start to look for them.

They are examples of common causes that create most accidents in the system. This knowledge will lead people to focus on fixing the system instead of striving to maintain the status quo by fixing the blame.

Here are some more real life examples of common causes that influence safety performance. (I'm sure the reader can add to the list.)

- Poor design and delivery of safety training to employees
- No data on how well safety training was understood and practiced by workers to help improve how training is delivered
- Poor design of training effort, training room uncomfortable, noisy, time constraints, interruptions during classroom sessions, poor lighting, people missing
- No follow-up on training to see how it is retained and applied
- Failure to remove the barriers that prevent workers from doing their job safely, i.e. the persecution of production that requires supervision choose between production vs. safety
- Poor relations between supervision and hourly employees
- Failure to measure the effects of common causes on safety and to reduce them

- Poor housekeeping practices that lead to poor attitudes toward management and peers
- Lunch rooms and break rooms that are filthy
- Heavy materials which are awkward to lift and place
- Methods and materials with uncontrolled or overexposed hazards
- Poor ergonomic designs of equipment and machinery for all employees
- Failure to use operational definitions of what it means to be safe
- Failure to apply the customer principle when it comes to safety
- Failure to apply systems thinking to safety management
- Dependency on mass safety inspections to hold workers accountable for common causes (things they can't control)
- The use of safety incentives to motivate workers to be safe
- Failure to provide standardized work methods
- Failure to improve standardized work methods
- Poor lighting by design or lack of maintenance
- Using safety regulations as the ultimate specifications for safety
- Settling for compliance with safety regulations as being "good enough"
- Belief that absence of a negative means you have a positive (If an operation had no accidents last month things must be OK.)
- Belief that if one person can do the job safe, everyone can to it and be safe
- Poor design of work area, work envelope
- Poor plant layout
- Wrong type of equipment and machinery for job
- Lack of equipment provided to do the job safely
- Failure to remove the barriers that rob the hourly worker of the right to be safe while doing his job
- Poor instruction and poor supervision – (Allowing situations to exist where supervision must choose between doing a job safely or doing it expediently)
- Failure to measure the effects of common causes, (poor training, maintenance of training, poor lighting, maintenance of equipment, replacement of wrong equipment, culture) and reduce them

- Uncomfortable working conditions, repetitive work requirements, high noise level, making it difficult to hear and concentrate, awkward handling of materials, tight traffic conditions, walk-ways
- Shift of management's emphasis/focus back and forth between quality, safety and productivity
- Failure to understand the interactions and variation that exist in a system that cause most accidents
- Lack of profound knowledge to understand when accidents are the net result of the system, not the individual

More things about the system

SPC — A new way of thinking about safety data

"I never guess. It is a capital mistake to theorize before one has data. Insensibly one begins to twist facts to suit theories, instead of theories to suit facts."
Sir Arthur Conan Doyle

"Statistical methods provide the only method of analysis to serve as a guide to the understanding of accidents and to their reduction." [17]

W. Edwards Deming

The theory of statistical process control (SPC) was developed by Dr. Walter A. Shewhart at Bell Labs in the latter part of the 1920's. Shewhart studied many different manufacturing processes and observed that all processes displayed variation. He looked at variability as either falling within limits set by chance or outside these limits. He then studied manufacturing processes and found they behaved somewhat differently than natural processes. He developed the theory and techniques of statistical process control to help people learn when a process is stable or out of control statistically.

The Hawthorne plant owned by Western Electric knew it had problems with uniformity of product and put forth best efforts but according to Deming these only messed things up more. Dr. Shewhart was called in to help the plant and the one thing he found was the managers at the plant always attributed a special cause to any unwanted variation in product when most of the time they were seeing variation due to common causes. Dr. Shewhart knew they would have been better off if they would just focus on improving the process. All they were doing was "tampering" with the system. Shewhart made a distinction between the two types of variation: assignable causes and chance causes. Dr. Deming popularized the terms special and common causes.

It was Shewhart who identified the two mistakes managers make when trying to improve a system:

> Mistake No. 1. To react to trouble as though it came from a special cause when it actually came from a common cause. An example of this would be a safety trainer blaming poor retention of what he taught to students because his classroom was too warm and uncomfortable when it was really due to his dull boring delivery of the subject matter.

> Mistake No. 2. To react to trouble as if it came from a common cause when actually it came from a special cause. The safety trainer might believe a particular student didn't learn much from his class because the power point show was out of focus when the student actually forgot his glasses and had difficulty reading the slides.

Dr. Deming pointed out that either mistake will lead to disappointment. You could say to yourself that from this day forward you will never make mistake No.1 and attribute all undesired results to common causes. That would be very simple but it would maximize your losses from making Mistake No. 2. Or, you could adopt the policy of never making mistake No. 2, and attribute all undesirable outcomes to special causes, which would maximize your loss of making Mistake No. 1.

SPC charts provide a common language between management and workers to help limit Mistakes 1 & 2 described above. The following is an example of why you need to use them for safety management.

Reacting to data

A few years ago a safety director called me and said her plant manager was ready to talk about a new approach to safety. What triggered this urgency? His plant had a sudden increase in the number of accidents which they documented on a run chart every month. The actual run chart is shown below.

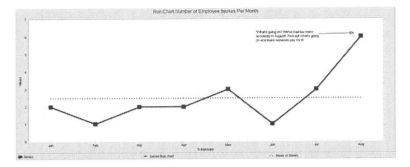

Run chart of accidents

The plant manager was very upset with what he considered a signal of something seriously wrong because of what happened in the month of August. I could only assume the number of accidents per month from January through July was acceptable to him. When he saw this surge he set up meetings with his supervisors to admonish them about their lack of diligence and commitment to safety in August. In fact he was late to our meeting because he was "chewing out" the supervisors about their poor safety performance in August. He couldn't put his finger on what it was exactly but he was determined to let his managers know they were going to be held accountable for it.

After a brief discussion with the plant manager it was apparent he was very knowledgeable about quality and the theory of statistical process control. Nonetheless, when we reviewed the run chart he pointed out the poor safety performance in August. It was a though he was proud of the fact he was taking safety seriously at this point.

Then I showed him the same accident data plotted on a control chart with upper control limits shown below. When he examined the C-Chart he was somewhat embarrassed. He knew immediately he had made a big mistake. With his knowledge of SPC he saw the uptick in August was not a special cause. It was just normal random variation or common cause variation. Statistically there was no difference between the performance in June with one accident and August when they had six!

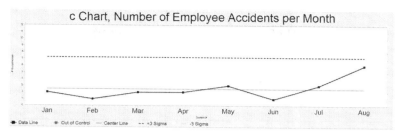

C Chart showing no special causes

The plant manager's initial reaction to the run chart is typical of how people who lack profound knowledge and understanding of statistical process control, respond to accident data. If a data point is negative they spend a lot of time and energy with their staff trying to figure out what caused it. This is exactly what the plant manager did. His managers couldn't explain what happened in August because they did not do anything different in August. They held all their safety meetings, performed all their safety inspections and investigated every accident the same as every month. They behaved the same way in months when they had only one accident.

The plant manager understood what the SPC chart was telling him and he realized his mistake immediately. He reacted as though something unusual had taken place in August. The C-Chart was telling him otherwise. Nothing was changed. The number of accidents was just a function of common cause variation. The way the plant managed safety they could expect the number of accidents to vary between o and 7 per month. The plant manager would have been making another mistake by congratulating his management team if the plant had "o" accidents one month. If he continued to react this way to each data point his managers would soon be totally confused and demoralized.

Although he was knowledgeable about SPC the plant manager hadn't thought about applying it to safety. Consequently, he made the mistake of blaming supervisors for what were common causes of variation built into the system. He was treating every data point as though it was the result of a special cause and losing the respect of his people.

To understand his mistake you must realize that if this were a chart representing scrap or defects and the operations had a good quality system, management would have reacted in the follow manner:

1.) First they would recognize the problem belongs to the system, not to some special cause. This would prevent them from blaming some individual employees or managers for the increase in the increase in August. The SPC chart shows there are no special causes and statistically the system is stable. More than likely the variation is due to common causes built into the system. Fixing the blame on someone will not fix the system.

2.) They would keep action focused on the system by having a team of workers take a deep dive into the operations and examine everything they could to understand what was causing the performance. Perhaps they would start with a pareto analysis and a flow chart. Then they would go to the area that is producing the most scrap or defects and observe what was happening.

3.) Then they would brainstorm as a team to develop innovative ways to reduce the number of defects or the amount of scrap.

4.) Then the team would implement their ideas and measure how they worked.

The one thing you must always remember about data concerning accidents. You are looking at what is called attribute data. It is a count of things gone wrong. Since every data point is an accident, (unless it is a zero) you know you have some trouble. The trick is to find out what kind of trouble you are dealing with. Does it come from the system or if it is from something local? That is how the language of SPC works as a powerful tool. It prevents a breakdown of communications and respect between management and workers.

In this particular case the manager made the typical mistake of treating a common cause as though it was a special cause. He was reacting to every data point on the chart as though it came from a special cause. His knee-jerk reaction was a series of meetings with his managers at which he berated them for their poor safety performance. He didn't take the time to analyze the data through the lens of profound knowledge and SPC. He was making the assumption all of the elements in the work system were OK and the people were just not doing what they were supposed to. The SPC chart made him realize his mistake. He was trying to fix the blame for a systems problem on some particular person or group of people and in doing so he was losing their respect.

Unfortunately, but predictably, his solution was first to chastise his manager and then to set up an incentive program to encourage workers to avoid having accidents. He didn't realize this would only encourage people to make the numbers look good. Since he believed the actions of employees were the major cause of accidents he assumed they just needed some extra motivation or incentive to work safer and the problem would be solved. Without any verification he assumed safety of the system was OK. How would he know any different?

I have yet to see or hear about management setting up a system to modify the behavior of employees as the methodology to solve a quality problem. You can't achieve better quality with slogans exhorting workers to "do it right the first time" or enticing them with incentives they can earn if they make parts with no defects. But these methods are routinely applied and viewed as acceptable solutions to just about any safety problem.

Clare Crawford-Mason, the producer of the 1980 documentary "If Japan Can...Why Can't We" who worked with Dr. Deming from that point on, says it took her ten years to understand the mindset he was describing. I've met managers from Ford Motor Company, who were trained personally by Deming that admitted to me they didn't know "what the hell the man was talking about."

I have to admit Deming's idea that statistical thinking is required for understanding accidents threw me for a loop. But as I learned more about statistical process control (SPC) and systems thinking it became clear. The proverbial light came on during a workshop when employees were describing a safety problem they wanted to correct.

As they drew the diagram below it dawned on me that they were dealing with variation of common causes, faults of variation in a system that interact that will ultimately cause an accident. This accident involved an employee being struck by a fork lift truck while doing her job at her work station. (No serious injury incurred.)

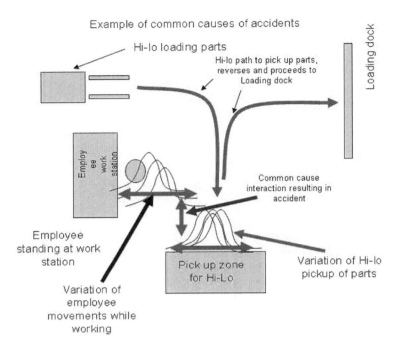

Example of common causes of accidents

The fork lift accident

As you can see, the fork lift driver has to maneuver his vehicle close to the worker to pick up parts. He cannot hit the pick up target exactly every time. There is going to be some variation. The employee at the work station is also moving to pick up parts and place them from her work station to the pick up zone. She will also have variation in her position. The initial accident investigation concluded the root cause was the unsafe actions of both the employee and the driver with more responsibility placed on the driver. As usual the employees agreed with the findings. What else could they say? Anyone with basic common sense would know to get out of the way of the vehicle and the driver is expected to watch out for pedestrians. The corrective action by recommended by management was to re-train both employees to obey safety rules, pay attention, watch out for each other and the driver was to sound the horn when entering and leaving the area.

But, when the workers and supervisors learned about profound knowledge, common causes, variation and the thinking of statistical process control they looked at the situation in another way and drew a very different conclusion. They could "see" how the common causes, faults of variation in the system and the design, were mostly responsible for the accident. (Variation and systems thinking) They understood the mindset of management (psychology) to maintain the status quo prevented them from improving the process. They could see if the system wasn't corrected another accident was very probable. (Knowledge and prediction) The common causes in the system itself had more to do with why an accident was going to happen than the actions of the individual workers. If anything, they were doing their best to avoid an injury by being careful! But eventually the random common cause variation would catch up with them.

The employees pointed out that if this was a quality problem and bad parts were being produced, they would have tried to error proof the process so it would never happen again. Instead they were forced to work in the system as it was and get the most out of it until one of them was almost seriously injured.

This is an example of how statistical thinking helps people understand accidents. They could see the common causes of accidents built into the system. Note: This new found knowledge doesn't relieve people from acting responsibly. It shows how a higher level of thinking brings a different perspective on how to solve safety problems. In this world it doesn't make sense to waste time trying to figure out who is to blame. It is much more productive to work on fixing the system.

The employees also realized management wasn't doing this on purpose. This setup was the result of relieving congestion in another area of the plant which meant they would have a difficult time changing it. (Push the system and it pushes back.) It's also another example of how a common cause can be misinterpreted as a special cause latter. This evaluation could apply to just about every accident in any operation.

As a result of the quality movement in the 1980's, U.S. manufacturers rediscovered the thinking of SPC. (U.S. manufacturers used SPC in the 1940's then abandoned it after WW II.) When they started using it again a lot of managers resisted. They thought it was an outmoded technique and it didn't apply to their particular operations. Their typical response was, "It won't work here, we're different." Of course this just wasn't true. SPC was applicable and it can be applied to any manufacturing or service business for both product and non-product systems. It can and should be an important method of safety management.

Critics of SPC for safety say that using SPC charts isn't appropriate because they are created after accidents happen. If that was true you couldn't use SPC for any kind of operation. They miss the point entirely. SPC is a way of thinking with tools attached. It is a language to be used by management and workers to study and improve the system.

You can't install SPC in an organization. It has to be embedded in the culture. For SPC to work people must learn how to be data driven and better problem solvers by applying the Plan, Do, Study and Act cycle. You must also understand the sun doesn't rise and set on SPC and data. SPC charts cannot exist in a vacuum. I've never seen nor heard of an SPC chart solving a problem. But they do help people do a better job of solving problems with a higher level of thinking and better understanding of the kinds of problems you are facing in your system.

To be effective SPC requires a new management paradigm. SPC charts help you predict how your system will behave in the future and indicate what kind of action is needed to fix the system. Knowledgeable teams using the charts will be able to interpret them properly and respond appropriately. If the culture of the company does not remove barriers that prevent proper use of the data and charts, as with any quality method, SPC is doomed. Learn as much as you can about SPC and apply it as it was meant to be used. As the two examples show you will open up an entirely new way of understanding accidents in your operations.

How the virus of variation affects safety

Work is a system of constant causes with sub systems of inputs, processes and outputs. These include planning, people, materials, methods, machinery, equipment and environment. As pointed out in the last section each part of the system has variation which creates common causes that can result in employee accidents. Myron Tribus calls this the virus of variability. [18]

Accidents that occur from common causes will occur by chance at unpredictable places and times but they may eventually display some stability and patterns. These patterns can be identified through statistical process control charts and a Pareto analysis. To change the outcomes of the system the interactions of variation of the parts of system have to be studied and controlled to achieve statistical control. In the context of SPC control means to restructure change.

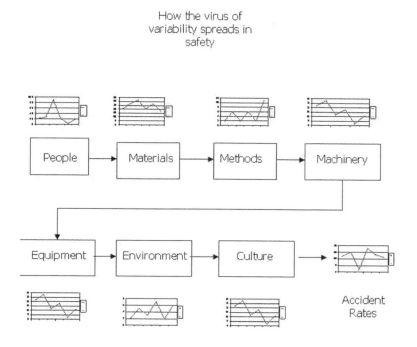

How common cause variation stacks up to cause accidents

Command and control managers start with the assumption that effort, or lack of it, on the part of the worker is what causes most of the safety problems in production. They have been taught most accidents are a result of special causes, things people do wrong. These are things they can see, things they can deal with. They don't appreciate how certain aspects of the system that can't be seen or easily recognized are connected and impact final outcomes. One of the most important aspects is variation.

To greater or lesser degrees, each part can and does have an influence on people in the system. Common causes interact randomly with each other. These interactions and their faults are like viruses and are a factor of why accidents happen. Just as you can't see a virus without the aid of a microscope; managers can't see these interactions without some type of assistance. Instead of a microscope, the tool to identify patterns of the outcome of the interactions is data.

How the virus of variation affects safety is fairly easy to describe. When it comes to safety you have many processes that make up your system. If you are the safety director you may have control over some and others you won't. You want to manage the system so you will get the very best safety performance. You know you will need the cooperation from all of the other departments, HR, Engineering, Production, Shipping and Receiving, etc. You want things to run smooth so no one will get injured but this is going to be very difficult.

In a way, Murphy's Law, if something can go wrong it will, applies at every interaction of the process. A tiny imperfection at any step can lead to another tiny misstep in another and that may affect another and so on. Eventually at some random point in the system something goes awry and an employee is injured. Congratulations, you now understand the interaction of forces or the Taguchi loss function as it applies to safety. Anything off target is a loss and these losses grow geometrically. An employee is subject to all of the losses of each process and these can lead to accidents. Variation in the system can work for you or against you.

For example, one way the virus of variation is introduced to the system is in safety training. Some people will learn more than others from a safety training class. You can have one person learn 95% of the subject matter and another only 60% from the same class. Yet both could conceivably be released to go to work. The virus exists in other things as well. For instance: the speed of the line, the number of breakdowns, the supervisor's mood. All have variation.

Let's say a department is having a pretty good day. The speed of the line is right on, the number of breakdowns has been low, the supervisor is in a good mood and the employee working in the area just happens to be the one who learned and retained all the essential information taught in the power lock out training class. A breakdown occurs and it requires maintenance of some equipment. The machine should be locked out to perform the work. What are the odds the lockout will take place? Well, in this case everything about variation in the system is working in your favor. You have a well trained employee, a happy supervisor not being pressed for production because the line has been running smoothly all day. The odds are pretty good the lockout will be performed, the repairs completed and no accidents will happen.

Let's change things a little bit. The next day you have an employee working in the area that only learned 50% of the lock out training and over time has forgotten 25% of that. The line is behind on production, the supervisor is in a lousy mood because of all the minor breakdowns incurred on this particular day. He is being pressed to get production because of the breakdowns. Now what are the chances for a lock out?

In this case the virus of variation is now working against you. The employee may not even remember that a lock out is required or if he does he may not remember how to do it properly. The supervisor has other pressing matters on his mind and is not in the mood to waste time on having the machinery locked out. The probabilities of the repair being done with the power locked out are not so good. If a lock out isn't performed and the employee is injured who do you think will be blamed for the accident? I have seen this situation happen many times over the years and I can assure you the injured employee and the safety department always gets the blame. People just won't be able to see that variation in the system itself has as much or more to do with the accident than anything else.

Ultimately, the symptom of the virus of variation is the number of accidents in operations. This is analogous to a fever brought on by a virus. The target temperature of the human body is approximately 98.6 Fahrenheit. Using a thermometer you can take a person's temperature to see how much of a difference exists between the target and the actual. The reading of the thermometer can't solve the problem or remove the virus. It just tells you how far off things are. Run charts, SPC charts, pareto charts, etc. serve the same purpose as a thermometer.

This is why the concept of statistical control is so important in safety management. We need to collect and analyze data that about variation that pertains to safety. For example we seek to standardize certain job methods so we can tell where the variation is coming from. This should be done for safety as well. A control chart can tell you if your safety system is stable, unstable, on or off target and if any special causes exist. It's also a fact an SPC chart does not solve the problems that create the variation. Only the people in an organization working together can do that. This is where your teams and the Plan, Do, Study and Act cycle come into play.

The Taylor/Heinrich model prevents using the thinking of statistical process control approach in three ways.

1. Most managers work from the premise 85% of accidents are caused by unsafe actions. This prevents them from attacking the virus of variation and applying systems thinking. When you start with the assumption the system is correct and if something goes wrong it's because someone has messed up you will focus on fixing the blame.

If we know anything about work systems it's the fact they do not run OK all of the time. There are always problems in one form or another. Single event thinking drives the Taylor/Heinrich model so your will never realize unsafe acts and conditions are actually symptoms of a management system infected by the virus of variation.

2. If you are dealing with a common cause, which is the majority of the time, your bias for believing people are responsible for most problems will lead you to treat it as a special cause. That means you will almost always react inappropriately. Do this and you will lose the respect of your people.

3. There is plenty of evidence to show traditional management has great difficulty fixing the system when things do not break. It's where the phrase, "If it ain't broke, don't fix it." comes from. The techniques used in command and control are designed to be applied as reactive, not proactive measures. Ironically a system can function with its common causes and their random variation and not have accidents for periods of time so management assumes things are OK even when they are not. This is called a false positive.

People working in a culture of continual improvement are always looking for way to improve the system. So even if you don't have accidents you will be wondering how other things that affect safety can be improved before things go wrong. You learn that absence of a negative doesn't mean you have a positive. For example; just because you had fewer or no accidents last month doesn't mean safety has actually been improved. It may just be normal variation with the common causes lining up to product that outcome.

When you understand how systems work and manage for continual improvement you realize waiting around for things to break or accidents to happen is actually a mistake. In the Taylor/Heinrich model when it comes to safety, "good enough" is acceptable and managers live by the credo "If it ain't broke don't fix it." They also ignore or deny variation exists. In continual improvement, "good enough" doesn't cut it and "no problem" is a problem. You will always be working on eliminating or reducing the virus of variation.

Intrinsic vs. Extrinsic motivation

Behind incentive programs lies managements patronizing and cynical set of assumptions about workers. Managers implicitly say to workers, I'm okay, you need incentives. Managers imply that their workers are withholding a certain amount of effort, waiting for it to be bribed out of them. Peter Scholtes

When it comes to safety, management spends a lot of time, money and resources trying to motivate employees to behave safely. Neo-Taylorism leads managers to believe employees simply lack the personal motivation to be careful at work.

Taylor laid the foundation for this way of thinking in his paper on Principles of Scientific Management. He said:

The remarkable and almost uniformly good results from the correct application of the task and the bonus must be seen to be appreciated.
These two elements, the task and the bonus (which, as has been pointed out in previous papers, can be applied in several ways), constitute two of the most important elements of the mechanism of scientific management.

The use of the bonus is one of Taylor's ideas we've retained but should have discarded long ago. Ever since Taylor management has put hourly workers on the motivation treadmill. Do this and you'll get that is believed to be if not the best, at least a certain way to make people behave the way you want. To most people's surprise the intense use of extrinsic motivators has been shown to diminish intrinsic motivation. In other words when you reward people for doing something you take away any personal interest they had for it in the first place. Unfortunately safety management with its emphasis on rewards to get workers to pay attention to safety has done great damage and disservice to the advancement of safety performance.

The exclusive reliance on extrinsic motivation has eliminated any opportunity for management to learn about and understand the power and benefits of intrinsic motivation. Especially when it comes to instilling pride and joy in work.

To simplify things intrinsic motivation is defined as doing something for its own sake. This is the opposite of extrinsic motivation which involves a person doing something and then expecting to receive something else as a result of participating in the activity.

You would be hard pressed to find a manager today who doesn't believe in and use some form of extrinsic motivation to encourage people to be more productive, sell more products or work safely. It's been said that no fact can overcome a prejudice, and the explosive hasn't been invented that can blow a totally wrong-headed idea out of a true believer's mind. The use of safety incentives is a perfect example of a wrong-headed idea fixated in the minds of managers and workers. The continued uncritical application of the use of extrinsic motivators to make people behave safely shows the limited knowledge and interest management has for learning what truly causes accidents.

Contrast this attitude with the new management model of continual improvement in which a basic principle is that people work for more than just a reward. The same managers that employ safety incentives know it is useless even silly to try to improve quality by just exhorting workers to "do it right the first time." We've known for years incentives have little or nothing to do with solving quality problems. A quality manager who would offer up incentives as the method to reduce defects and scrap would probably have a short lived career. Not that is hasn't been tried. We've learned unequivocally to improve quality everyone must work on improving the system. Relying on incentives to reduce and eliminate quality defects is just plain dumb. The quality of your parts or service is the outcome of the processes in your system. To improve quality you must improve the system with the help of the workers. This was proven years ago with quality circles.

Safety and accidents are equivalent to quality and defects. Both are the outcomes of the management system. The obvious question is; if you can't reduce scrap or defects with rewards and incentives why would they help reduce employee accidents?

Yet it's quite common for managers to rely on incentive or reward programs as a legitimate activity to improve safety. They honestly believe using extrinsic motivators is an effective solution to prevent employee accidents. It's another example of how non-systems thinking managers focus on fixing the person, not the system. Now that you've learned about Taylor and Heinrich you can now understand why they think this way.

Over the years we seemed to have confused manipulating people with motivating them. If you want someone to perform a task, especially one that is repetitive and mind-numbing, you will have problems finding people to do it. But, as Taylor pointed out, you can always offer them something like more money. This isn't motivating them but seducing them to do something you want by offering them something to do it. We commonly call this a bribe.

We need to understand the difference between using incentives and creating a company with a positive constructive culture where people will contribute willingly to the company's success. In his book, *Punished by Rewards*, Alfie Kohn, a leading expert on the use of incentives, reveals that in the short and long term, incentives really don't work the way we would like. In fact, more often than not their impact is exactly the opposite of what you want to happen. Alfie offers the compelling argument, backed by extensive research that the quality of performance and the interest people have in doing something for its own sake declines when rewards are used. Peter Scholtes, another quality guru, says flat out managers cannot motivate people. He says the carrot and stick approach was developed for use with jackasses and it can be applied successfully only to that species. [19]

Nonetheless everyday in America managers and consultants try to improve safety using incentives, rewards or positive reinforcement to employees who behave safely and do not have accidents. Which begs the question, why does management think people lack the motivation to work safely in the first place? The only answer that makes sense is that's what they have been taught to think. They continue to do it in spite of the fact people are fully self-motivated not to get injured. A quote from an employee in one of my workshop says it all, *"This company doesn't pay me enough to hurt myself."*

Since the 1970's management has come to realize that people don't come to work to purposely make some scrap. They also rediscovered quality theory. As a result managers had to stop blaming workers for defects made in the system. Most management will concede that people don't come to work with the intention of making scrap or injuring themselves. Human beings have a built-in defense mechanism for self-preservation. Under normal circumstances intrinsic motivation combined with common sense works quite well to protect us from obvious hazards we encounter in our every day experience.

The fact is a work system and its processes have many different types of hazards. Therefore, it is management's responsibility to design, build and run the system so people can operate in it without fear of being injured. Work systems and processes are loaded with known and unknown hazards. Some are actually error inducing. It is not acceptable for management to rely on a person's common sense to protect them from hazards they will encounter on-the-job.

Management has learned to error-proof a job so the worker cannot make a defective part. Why doesn't management 'safety-proof' jobs so accidents can't occur? The answer is, they can and they do when it is easy, simple and cheap to do so. But safety proofing stops at a certain point; when management doesn't see the cost benefit.

If accidents persist after management has made some effort to prevent them the problem solving effort hits the wall. They get to the point where they just won't spend any more time or money to figure out how to stop accidents. Rather than keep working on the problem, as they would do for quality, they get frustrated, give up and put the responsibility for safety on the workers. It's at that point they typically roll out an incentive program.

In essence management is saying we can't figure out a way to solve this safety problem and can't afford to spend any more time and money on it. So we are leaving it up to you the employee to watch out for yourself. To help you stay alert and pay attention we will give you a little extra cash if you can avoid getting hurt. If for some reason you can't avoid getting injured you won't get the money and will probably be reprimanded. Surprisingly this approach starts to reduce an employee's intrinsic motivation to be safe.

In the Taylor/Heinrich model people's intrinsic motivation to work safe and do a good job is eliminated through the use of extrinsic motivators. Eventually employees will stop "thinking" about safety and start to worry more about how to get rewards. Management is laying the groundwork for employees to fail, to have accidents, because they've learned it doesn't pay to think. Then when accidents do happen, managers ask, why didn't the employee think? They don't understand, the system they created has taught employees to leave their ability to think in the parking lot because they won't need it while they are working. Management has done all the thinking for them.

Rewarding people for things they do for sheer pleasure or personal achievement is called overjustification. At best it is meaningless and a source of discouragement. At worst it will actual destroy the interest people have in doing something they previously did willingly on their own. In the situation described above that would include the employee working with management to solve whatever the insoluble safety problem is.

Alfie Kohn tells a story about ten-year old kids who walk by an old man's house each day and yell insults at him about being ugly and bald. One afternoon the old man comes up with a plan. He waits for them at his front fence and offers to pay a dollar to each one that comes by the next day and yells rude comments at him. Amazed and excited, sure enough the next day the kids show up early and yell insults at him for all they're worth. The old man pays up and tells the kid to do the same the next day and he will pay each of them twenty-five cents. The kids thought that was still pretty good so they show up again the next day and taunt him. He pays them off in quarters but then announces he can only pay them a penny the next day. The kids look at each other in disbelief "A penny?" they repeat scornfully. "Forget it!" And they never come back again.

The old man had an elegant solution to his problem. By rewarding the kids for doing something they were doing voluntarily, something they thought was fun, they came to see themselves as harassing him in order to get paid. As soon as the reward was gone so were they. They started out doing something for nothing and were enjoying it. (Although it was mean.) It ends up that the rewards destroyed their intrinsic motivation. When the reward was removed they stopped doing something they were doing initially for their own satisfaction. The old man killed their interest in doing something they enjoyed doing for free in the first place.

Why would you expect any other outcome from safety incentives or rewards? People start out being interested in safety. They will work diligently without any extra payment to help management prevent accidents. Management learns about safety problems they either can't solve or want to spend resources on. Instead they decide to start an incentive program and rewards employees that work with no injuries. Of course employees that do get injured do not get any rewards. (They get punished twice.) At some point, as they always do, the incentive program stops. What do you think happens?

Start rewarding employees for working safely, which is something people are more than happy to do in the first place, and you will do just what the old man did to the kids. Kill their interest in it.

Capturing the hearts and minds of people

"Successful enterprises create the conditions to allow their employees to do their best work. Companies should treat employees like their most valuable resources, including pushing decision making to the lowest levels." Peter Drucker

When you look any traditionally managed safety program it becomes readily apparent that management is trying to solve safety problems from its own point of view. They use the system to act on the workers usually with the help of the latest fad presented by the human resources department. But if you are going to fix safety problems you must try to solve them from the point of view of the workers. They are the true safety customers and they face the safety issues on-the-job every day. To improve safety you will need to capture their hearts and minds.

One thing I have learned is that to make any safety effort effective it's imperative all employees to own it. Dr. Norman Maier, a research and consulting psychologist, recognized that effective decisions are the products of the quality of thinking multiplied by the acceptance of the decision by the people who have to implement it. This is an important formula for the successful implementation of an idea in any organization.

$$ED = Qt \times A$$

Effective Decisions = Quality of Thinking X Acceptance

Companies often ignore the wisdom of this equation and seek the advice of outside experts to devise solutions to a safety problem. They may be specialists employed in the company or outside consultants. I use a hypothetical situation to demonstrate how this plays out. Let's suppose employees are getting foreign bodies in their eyes at a particular work station. An outside expert is hired and his solution is to have the workers wear hoods designed to cover the workers heads. They are equipped with a glass window so they can see out of the hoods. These hoods will provide 100% protection of the eyes so there is no chance of any type of material even getting close to the eyes of the workers. The quality of her solution is a 10 with 10 being the best rating. The hoods will protect the workers from getting something in their eyes 100%. But, will the workers wear them? The answer to this question on the same scale would probably be a 1 or 2.

$$10 \times 2 = 20$$

Now change the situation so the workers are asked to find a solution themselves. They form a team to investigate and decide they want to find some protective glasses that meet all safety standards and are well designed. (They can do this because they've practiced how to work as a team many times before they attack the problem.) They find a local company that makes safety glasses that are very comfortable and are quite fashionable. They have safety side shields form fitted to each individual. They won't guarantee 100% protection but they will do the job quite well. Let's say they will protect the workers 90% as well as the hoods.

In this case the workers who are impacted by the situation are used to come up with a viable solution. Now what does the result of the equation show? As far as the quality of the decision to use the safety glasses you would give it a 9. But the main difference is in the acceptance of wearing the glasses. Their commitment (acceptance) could be a 7. The equation now looks like this:

$$9 \times 7 = 63$$

Which is the better solution? Obviously, the latter since you have a gain of 63 vs. only 20 in the first example. When teams have input and control, it creates true ownership of the solution.

In a throwback to Taylorism, safety management often assigns the thinking process to an expert when it would be much better to use the minds of the workers to study and solve the safety problem. Of course, management should make sure the worker's have been trained in team problem solving skills so they are equipped to meet the challenge they are being asked to face.

In the Taylor/Heinrich model management sets up the system and the workers must do what they're told. For safety the main objective is for employees to follow the safety rules. It may work for a time, but the price you pay is dear. The most glaring problem is the destruction of respect for management by the workers and things go downhill from there.

People won't be highly committed to safety if they don't have a voice in the decisions about how safety affects them. With it emphasis on rules and regulations and dependence on command and control traditional safety programs have a tendency to foster the adult/child relationship by treating workers as children then expecting them to behave as adults. Most traditional safety managers fret over how to hold workers accountable for complying with safety rules and regulations. They don't understand that people on teams willingly hold themselves accountable because they own the safety process. Ownership of safety instills pride in work. Ownership creates commitment and commitment creates people who will work with management to improve safety every day. Ownership eliminates the need for management to worry about who is going to be held accountable.

Take fear out of safety

A committee appointed by the President of a company will report what the President wishes to hear. Would they dare report otherwise? From The New Economics

Managers at California's largest nuclear plant won safety bonuses for years by hiding employees' on-the-job injuries and dodging state reporting rules, it was reported Friday. In testimony during nine days of regulatory hearings this month, employees of the San Onofre Nuclear Generating Station alleged the utility deliberately covered up employee injuries in order to win safety bonuses, according to the Los Angeles Times

There may be no greater loss to a company than the losses created by fear. People who are afraid they are going to get blamed for an accident harbor feelings of anxiety, mistrust, opposition and secrecy. In management, fear creates an atmosphere where people play politics, lie and resort to backstabbing. This is not the culture needed to foster teamwork and cooperation which are necessary for effective problem solving. Fear comes in many forms. It can range from brute force management to subtle policies and procedures of bureaucracy. There is no place for management by fear anywhere in the system of managing for continual improvement. The cost of employing fear in the name of safety is immeasurable. Blaming people for an accident and creating fear has never solved any safety problem or improved any process.

One example of management by fear; people are told to get the numbers or else. They're not told what "or else" means but they can figure out it isn't going to be anything good. When this happens people will somehow get the numbers. The pressure of top management's desires will instill fear in any organization and the numbers will turn out to be what management wants to hear. When management takes this posture for safety, people become afraid to report safety problems, which include injuries. There have been many instances of companies being cited by regulators for falsifying safety data. There's plenty of evidence to support Dr. Deming's fifth principle that recognizes there will always be accidents, none to refute it. It doesn't mean you don't try to prevent all of them. But the methods you use will be much different than those advocated by Taylor/Heinrich, a lot of which ultimately instill fear in the employees.

A company I worked with was trying to find out exactly what was happening regarding safety problems in the field. Management asked workers to report any near hits they experienced while working. At the end of the first month only a few reports came in and they were from the safety committee. None of the other employees reported any safety problems a highly unlikely situation.

When questioned about the lack of reports, the employees said there was no way they were going to tell management about any safety problems. Not because they didn't exist but because they believed doing so would jeopardize their jobs. This was in spite of the fact no one had ever received a reprimand for reporting a safety problem in the past. The owner met with every employee, gave them his personal assurance and a signed letter stating no reprimands would be issued for reporting near hits. He explained he just wanted to get the data about safety on-the-job. It took over 3 months to convince employees they would not be reprimanded for telling management about safety issues they faced on the job! And this was a company that didn't employee fear! Evidently the employees had experienced the same scenario at previous employers and couldn't believe management wouldn't use the data against them.

Recently, a client whose management was trying hard to transform its philosophy had an accident in their plant operations. It involved a powered industrial truck that hit a pedestrian. Fortunately, no one was seriously injured. Unfortunately they fell back into their old habits and conducted an accident investigation immediately. The driver passed a post accident drug test and was properly licensed for the vehicle. He was in good standing with a good attendance record. While he was backing up the vehicle another employee, partially hidden from view and not normally expected to be working in the area, walked behind the vehicle. The driver backed into the area and bumped the employee. The area was congested and the plant is rather noisy.

Management decided the proper action was to discharge the driver of the powered industrial truck. (He was later reinstated after the union filed a grievance, but this was after he lost two weeks of pay, just before Christmas.) When I asked the Human Resource manager why they fired the driver his response was they had to show the union that management was serious about safety. And he had to protect himself in the event of any future accidents because the staff from headquarters would expect this type of response.

When I asked him what he meant by protecting himself, he explained if this type of accident happened again he was afraid of what his corporate staff would do. He was not going to take any chances that would make them unhappy. He reprimanded the driver and documented it in his personnel file. If he didn't do this he believed his own job might be in peril. (I only wish people would take this "if only" approach before an accident happened.)

Incredibly, this same manager had recently told me he ascribed to Deming's teachings and tried to practice them. He didn't understand that by taking this action he was actually planning for more accidents, not preventing them. Instead of driving fear out of the organization he was a employing it and being victimized by it at the same time. He destroyed the trust we were trying to build between management and the hourly employees. He also showed his own fear and lack of leadership by reacting as he did to the potential threat of his corporate bosses. What else could he do? Similar scenarios take place in plants throughout the U.S. everyday.

The last and one of the most blatant examples of how management employs the subtle use of fear on employees is the argument that safety is mostly a matter of employees making personal choices. This angle of the use of fear comes from the minds of marketing professionals to help sell products and services to improve safety that rely exclusively on changing the behavior of workers. In this scenario the assumption is it is perfectly reasonable to hold employees responsible for making the correct choice at the right moment to prevent an accident. This is in spite of the fact all kinds of other things may have been wrong up to that point.

You would have to be living under a rock not to know that employees have little or no control over how they perform most of their work processes. It may sound reasonable to expect employees to make the right choice about safety until you bring all the factors of command and control management to bear on how employees are instructed to do their job. And that is to follow procedures and not think about what they are doing.

Blaming people for mistakes or things gone wrong is a symptom of a management by fear. Fear, no matter what form it comes in, destroys teamwork and trust which prevents continual improvement. A mistake is not a crime, and a crime is not a mistake. You have to know the difference between the two and honor that.

Part 5

Methods and tools for CRISP

The aim of Part 5 is to introduce some new methods to manage safety systems and show how they can be used by managers and employees to examine and correct the system. These activities should replace traditional safety management activities such as mass safety inspections, accident investigations and incentive programs.

Using the customer focus for safety

Any company that does not focus on satisfying its customers will not be in business for long. Truly successful companies know this and they live and die by the philosophy that taking care of the customer is the number one priority. You can tell the companies who really mean it when they say the customer comes first. Their employees know how to serve customers and do it every day. They are employed for their mental as well as their manual labor. They are called knowledge workers.

Peter Drucker said knowledge workers should be managed as though they are volunteers. They have skills and are very mobile. In the past employees might work for a company all their working lives and retire with a gold watch. Now people can expect to work for many different companies in their careers. They can also expect many different changes in what they will have to learn to stay employed. One of the most important skills they will have to learn is to take care of customers.

In the Taylor/Heinrich model the foremost goal of safety management was to please the Voice of the Boss or the Voice of the Regulator. Safety management must realize it is not immune to the drastic change demanded of job skills in the new economy. The biggest difference will be the recognition that employees are the most important customers of safety. When this happens the focus of safety management will shift from working to satisfy the safety regulators by complying with safety standards, to ensuring the safety needs of workers are met. Safety must learn how to apply the customer principle.

In business a customer is defined as anyone who benefits from your product or service. Quality departments have long recognized a company has both internal and external customers. Each operation in the line of production is a customer. Employees obviously benefit from the safety designed and delivered to them in their operation. Hence they are first and foremost *the most important customers* of safety in any organization.

There are supplier-customer links in all business processes. In this system the next operation is your customer. This sets up the supplier-customer linkage which creates a chain throughout the processes in any company. It goes something like this:

Supplier A   Customer of Supplier A
uses   then they perform   receives
inputs   operations and pass   output from Supplier A
               to next customer   and they become Supplier B:

Supplier B   Customer of B
who uses   then they perform   who receives their
inputs   operations and pass to output (and so on)

In business, you are always either a supplier or a customer. It just depends on what you are doing at the time. So each and every employee in a company at some point is a customer of the safety department. If safety is doing its job, each employee becomes a better supplier for the company as a result of their interaction with the safety department.

Another important aspect about the customer principle for safety is discovered in the answer to the question, who defines quality? Companies have learned the only real opinion that counts when it comes to defining quality is that of the customer. Customers define quality. They do so with their pocketbook. Besides the ultimate customer who pays for products and services, who knows more about quality problems than anyone else? The answer: the person doing the job.

When you apply the customer principle to safety you must ask the question, who defines whether a job is safe? The answer is; the person who does the job, not just the regulator or the boss as is typically the case in the Taylor/Heinrich model. When it comes to safety, this answer changes everything. Business spares no effort trying to satisfy the needs and expectations of its customers. No less of an effort should be taken when it comes to taking care of safety customers.

Traditionally, the primary goal for safety has been to ensure the company meets the safety specifications, rules and regulations promulgated by management and outside regulatory agencies. This includes regulators such as OSHA, EPA, etc. It would be a pretty safe bet that if OSHA were dismantled over half of all safety directors' jobs would disappear rather quickly. It's not because safety would no longer be a concern, but the work they do is mainly to ensure the company has complied with safety regulations. An employee in one of my workshops pointed out correctly that regulators are non-elective suppliers to safety management, not direct customers.

The obvious question is, who knows more about safety problems on-the-job than anyone else? The answer is; the person doing the job. So why don't we recognize this reality and work to get the Voice of the Safety Customer into the Voice of the Process, as we do in quality?

To do so the safety department, or whoever is responsible for safety in your organization, should answer the following questions:

When it comes to safety –
Who are your customers?
What do they want?
What are their needs?
How will you know they are satisfied?

The quest for identifying safety customers starts with drawing a customer safety map. This exercise forces you to think about your safety customers and put their needs at the forefront of your safety management system. The map below is an example of a customer map for safety.

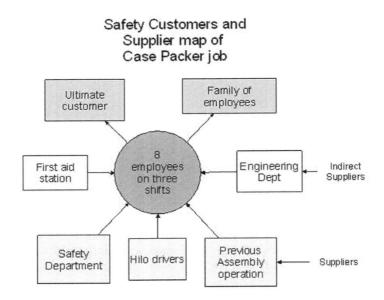

A safety customer map

Everything about safety in every organization should start from the customer principle. If you do this you will never have managers treating safety as an afterthought. The way to truly make safety important to your company is to apply the customer principle to safety. It changes the fundamental reason why safety exists in a company.

Operational definitions

> *"What we have...is failure to communicate."* Strother Martin, a scene from the movie, Cool Hand Luke.

> *"In my opinion, the mine was safe."* Statement by Ben Hatfield, CEO of ICG, commenting on the fact that 17 of the 208 alleged safety violations against the company issued by Mine Safety and Health Administration were classified as serious. An explosion in the mine killed 12 employees just two weeks before.

> *"In the opinion of many people in industry, there is nothing more important for the transaction of business than the use of operational definitions. It could also be said nothing is more neglected."*
> W. Edwards Deming

The customer principle is the most important reason for safety to exist. The use of operational definitions is next. Although their importance cannot be denied they are seldom if ever used. Very few people, even those trained in quality methods, have the faintest idea of what an operational definition is, why they are important or how to make one.

The word *safe*, like *quality*, can be difficult to define. Managers, workers, safety inspectors and anyone else involved in a job have their own viewpoint of whether a particular job is "safe." Mr. Hatfield's quote above is an obvious example of how one person's definition does not correspond with another's. If a supervisor is task oriented, and almost all of them are, she will not take the workers viewpoint about safety into consideration. Her primary concern is to get parts made or keep production going. As long as the job meets safety specifications, that is probably all she is worried about. If a worker does get injured, it's unfortunate, but the employee must be held accountable because at the time of the accident the supervisor believed the job was "safe."

Systems thinkers understand the need for a tool to help people agree about concepts and adjectives. This is especially true about transactions between a supplier and a customer. Who defines quality? We've learned the only definition of quality that's important is the customer's. A business must constantly strive to understand the Voice of the Customer. If a company's product or service does not include the customer's requirements they will lose customers and go out of business.

Operational definitions are one of the best tools to get the Voice of the Customer into the Voice of the System. A supervisor and a worker will often have different opinions on whether or not a job is safe. Operational definitions are the tool to ensure all parties agree that a word means the same thing to everyone. They provide the method of communicating the same meaning of a word, concept or idea between two or more people. Operational definitions are not what you intended but what you actually receive.

How many companies have issued a safety policy from top management stating they want all operations to be safe yet accidents continue to happen? The president of the company makes a proclamation that he wants all employees to be "safe." His safety policy is dutifully broadcast throughout the organization; first to upper management typically vice presidents, then to the plant managers, then to supervisors and they tell the workers how important it is for the company's operations to be "safe." Over the years whenever I ask an audience if they think "safe" means the same thing to the president, vice presidents, managers, supervisors and the hourly employees of the company the overwhelming answer is "No." Then I ask, should it? And the overwhelming response is "Yes."

The word "safe" often has a different meaning to different people in the same company. It's quite obvious the families of the miners who lost their lives at the Sago mine would take issue with Mr. Hatfield and his definition of whether the mine was "safe."

As I said earlier, an operational definition is what actually happens, not what was intended. At the end of the year a company can measure its safety performance and the result is the operational definition of safety. For example, if a company had an incident rate of 3.5 per hundred employees with 15 lost time injuries, like it or not, that is the operational definition of safe. It is what the safety effort of company operations delivered. Management may make a publicly state its safety goal is zero accidents but that is only a goal not a result.

Any definition exists solely in the minds of the people that make it. To be useful words like tired, soft, round, reliable, good only have meaning when expressed in operational terms. The concept of a definition cannot be expressed in words. How do you define the color blue? Does everyone see exactly the same thing when they look at something that is blue? What one person sees as beautiful may be totally ugly to someone else. Two people may watch a movie and both have different opinions about how "good" it was. Management may think a specific job is safe, but the employees that do the actual work may disagree with them. This leads to many problems, misunderstandings and unnecessary employee injuries.

An operational definition is one that reasonable people can agree on. When you have a specification, standard operating procedure, instruction, measure or regulation being used by two or more people, you will need an operational definition so everyone can agree on what it means. Without an operational definition specifications can be rendered meaningless.

For example, let's say a safety regulation requires a "competent person" be present at a job site. (There has actually been such a requirement.) What does "competent person" mean? Competent to run equipment, train other employees, converse with the inspector? Read and understand at a fifth grade level? Could someone who is less competent do a better job? Could you define less competent? One could only conclude that the regulation has no meaning. The supervisor may think the person he assigned to run the job is perfectly competent but an OSHA inspector may consider the same person totally incompetent.

Every top executive will say they want all operations to be a "safe place to work." Yet every company has accidents on a continual basis. So what do these executives mean when they use the word safe? Safe at the beginning, during or end of the shift? Does "safe" mean the same thing to the foreman? to the workers? to safety inspectors? Does "safe" mean the same thing on a monthly, weekly, daily or hourly basis? Or does the meaning of safe change with the demands of production? This is one of the biggest problems with safety in a task oriented company. Safety is a moving target. You can't always see it so it is difficult to hit.

Without an operational definition, safety specifications, job safety analysis, safety procedures can have very different meanings depending on who is interpreting them. When an operation must be safe, safe should mean the same to the worker, to the foreman, to the inspector and top management yesterday, today and in the future.

To create an operational definition you must always determine what is the purpose? Of course it will depend on who's asking. Is it to keep the regulator happy or keep the worker from having an injury? Each purpose has unique criteria. This means you will have a different test method for each one. And for each test we will get a different answer. (Deming seemed to get a kick out of the fact we get different numbers for the speed of light depending on how we measure it.) Once you have completed your test you can determine if you have met your criteria and provide a Yes or No answer. With an operational definition a job is either safe or it is not safe. There's no in between or grey areas.

| Question: | Is the operation safe? |
| For what purpose? (Criteria) | For the number of recordable injuries |

| Test method: | Count the number of recordable injuries on the log at the end of each month. If we have any recordable injuries the operation is not safe. |
| Decide | Yes or No |

Question:	Is the operation safe?
For what purpose?	
(Criteria)	For an OSHA audit
Test method:	Number of serious violations observed during safety inspections each week. If we have any "serious" violations noted from inspections the operation is not safe.
Decide	Yes or No

None of these operational definitions are wrong but they could all deliver different results. It depends on what world you are working in whether or not they work for you. There have been many instances of operations that met safety codes but employees were still injured. Unfortunately, many companies consider outside safety regulators as the safety customer and use only their criteria to define safe.

Operational definitions provide a clear, concise and detailed definition of a measure. If a measure is only important to one person you probably don't need an operational definition. When two or more people are involved in a measure or a specification, i.e. a customer and a supplier or a safety inspector and a worker, then an operational definition is in order. That way, everyone involved in the process outcomes can agree on the results achieved.

Lack of operational definitions at work can really cause safety problems. Consider the following excerpt from an actual company safety policy statement:

"The company shall establish comprehensive and realistic policies based on past experience and current scientific research to prevent unreasonable health and quality/safety risks."

What does *"realistic policies"* mean? What are *unreasonable health and safety risks*? Does this apply to actual work processes? Realistic policies for whom? the plant manager? the foreman? or the workers? who? This statement is nothing more than a public relations effort. It sounds good, but it can mean just about anything you want it to.

Very few top managers see what happens to safety when the job runs. They depend on others in the company to worry about whether or not the job is "safe." Consequently, what top management wants and what they receive are often two very different things.

How is an operational definition made? Start with a question. For instance: Is the loading job "Safe?" To make an operational definition you must also ask, what is your purpose?

1. Why are you creating the operational definition? What is your purpose?

    We have decided the purpose is: To determine if the loading job is safe.

2. Then identify the critical characteristic.

    You then have to identify the critical characteristic you associate with the process safety measure(s). Our goal is to reduce the number of wrist injuries when doing the loading job so the critical characteristic is "strains to the wrists that cause discomfort during a work shift on the loading job." The key word in the criterion is "discomfort." You can stretch your wrists a certain amount with no discomfort. However, repetitive stretching of the wrist too far will cause discomfort that can lead to pain and eventually a workers compensation claim. In other words stretching your wrists that does not cause "discomfort" is not to be counted. Such distinctions are critical to operational definitions so they will be consistent and understood by everyone involved.

3. Select how you will measure the characteristic of interest.

    In our example we will count the *number of strains that cause discomfort to the wrist* by getting feedback from the employees who do the loading job to record any of these strains with discomfort to the wrist on a check sheet.

4.   Describe the test method

The test method is the actual procedure for taking the measurement. This includes the "where" and "how" the measurement will be taken. You must select an appropriate way to measure the characteristic of interest. In this example a check sheet will be located at the work station and employees will put a mark on the sheet if they experience any discomfort to their wrist during a work shift.

5.   State the judgment criterion or criteria

Judgment criteria allow you to make a decision about the characteristic of interest. Does it exist—yes or no? There should be no in between. The job is either safe or it is not safe.

In our example the decision criterion says to have employees mark the number of "strains that cause discomfort to the wrists" during their shift. Therefore, if any employee records discomfort to the wrist, the operation would not be "safe."

5.   Document the operational definition

You should always document the operational definition. They can be useful for standardizing training manuals and job procedures.

In our example, this process is not "safe" if any discomfort to the wrist is reported. The people working in the area should determine if the discomfort stems from common or special causes. Note the operational definition doesn't provide a solution to the problem. It just helps everyone agree you've got a problem.

Teams and safety management

...It is obvious teams outperform individuals...It is not obvious how top management can exploit that advantage. The potential impact of single teams, as well as the collective impact of many teams, on the performance of large organizations is woefully underexploited. From the book, The Wisdom of Teams

Team learning is vital because teams not individuals, are the fundamental learning unit in modern organizations. This is where the "rubber meets the road"; unless teams can learn, the organization cannot learn. From the book – The Fifth Discipline

The lack of understanding about teams and resistance to teamwork by American managers at this stage of the game is truly mind boggling. American managers have been learning about teamwork since the 1970's. I seriously doubt there is a manager or supervisor in the United States who hasn't been through some sort of team training and has led some sort of team. The team concept in American companies has been sliced and diced and served up many different ways but with no real recipe for sustained success. Just about every other company can point to some successful use of teams at some point in time in their operations. But very few have been able to sustain true team management. It's a sad state of affairs but it is a fact.

One of the reasons teams don't flourish is command and control management is still the dominant management method. We have softened its presentation but managers still adhere to its basic principles. One of those is to view the system as a given that is not to be touched. Managers believe their job is to get everything they can out of the system. For this they don't need the help of the workers on teams. In their world productivity is improved by directing the workers to do what management wants. They believe outputs are a direct result of what managers desire and direct. These managers believe most problems stem from people not following their directions.

They will occasionally use teams for a number of reasons, none of which tap the serious potential of team problem solving and decision making. They are mostly ad hoc applications that managers point to as examples of their commitment to teamwork. But there is no solid evidence of companies transforming from command and control methods to true team management. Companies can only show micro applications where employees may form a team and work on one specific problem with varying results. When the work is done or project completed the teams are quickly abandoned with little effort to keep them working as a true entity managing daily work routines on a continual basis. Management always returns to impart its role of managing employees through various command and control techniques.

The bottom line is, teams and teamwork just don't fit with command and control management theory. Teams are useful to command and control managers and they will use them when they are in a jam. But when it comes to handing over the reins and allowing teams to really run things, forget about it. A manager steeped in Taylorism or Neo-Taylorism is not going to let that happen. He just cannot give up his power or believe hourly workers know more about business than he does. When teams come to this type of manager with their solutions he will respond with comments such as:

- I'm not sure that will work. Go back and do it over.
- You are empowered but check with me before you do anything.
- We can't put that idea into use because there is nothing the budget for it.
- We've tried something like that before. I don't think it will work.
- The job is only going to last a few more months. We can't spend any money improving things now.

With all of the talk about teams and teamwork the fact is, American managers still have limited knowledge, experience and ability about how to lead, train and manage teams. The management infrastructure to support and sustain teams doesn't exist. Even the most progressive companies have great difficulty making teams work over time. There are just too many remnants of command and control management to prevent them from working effectively. As long as there are performance appraisals, emphasis on internal competition and incentive programs, teams cannot and will not be able to achieve their true potential.

Having said that it doesn't mean using teams is futile. You will be able to use them but you must learn how and when they will work in your organization. Safety management has almost completely ignored the power and ability of teams to work on and solve safety problems. When it's convenient, companies will use teams to address safety problems. They will have the occasional Kaizen blitz or set up an ergonomic team to work on one specific problem. But the use of teams as an integral management tool to manage safety on a daily basis really isn't on the radar screen.

The fact is teams should be the fundamental management approach for safety. As I have been pointing out throughout this book, safety problems are almost always system problems and systems are almost always too complex to be understood by just one person. It takes a well trained team to solve them. As Senge says, teams are the building blocks of organizational learning. This applies 100% to safety.

So how can a business exploit the ability of people to work on a team and solve a safety problem? The answer, it will have to train its people, especially middle managers and workers on the skills necessary to lead and manage teams. In most instances this means it will have to change its culture.

I was introduced to teams in the 1970's, the peak of white collar think and blue collar do culture. One manager described this era as "command and controls times ten." An hourly employee's only responsibility was to do what they were told, when they were told to do it. As a manager I had no reason to worry about working on or leading a team. They didn't exist.

I was introduced to the team concept while working with the local safety council. A gentleman approached me after one of my presentations and asked if I had ever used teams to address safety problems. He offered to demonstrate some team building/problem solving instruments. He put me and my staff through a simple exercise that proved the effectiveness of teams. The session was interesting and a lot of fun. It was the start of my long learning curve about teams which continues to this day. The exercises were developed by the late Dr. Clay Lafferty and I've been using and learning from them ever since.

The outstanding thing about the training exercises was that they provided a comparison between an individual and the team solution. They give a statistically valid evaluation of the two opinions. The bottom line was, after you completed the exercise you could see if your team worked together effectively when solving a problem. It's one thing for people to say they work well as a team. It's quite another to prove it.

I use graphs to show the gain or loss by the team compared to the individual scores. Over the years the data shows approximately 85% or more of the time teams come up with better solutions than individuals. I was skeptical about this premise before I discovered the exercises.

But the data was undeniable. They proved time after time teamwork is the way to go when working on system problems. I realized it would be irresponsible not to use teams to solve safety problems at work. The evidence is just too compelling.

I started using the team building exercises with companies just to see how they would be received. It was a real eye-opener. People would come up to me after these safety meetings and ask if they could have copies of the instruments so they could take them home to do with their family. Imagine that! I never had anybody do anything like that in any other safety meeting. It was another example of the Hawthorne effect identified in the 1920's at the Western Electric plant where Shewhart worked. Studies at the plant showed if management paid any kind of attention to workers productivity went up. We need to act on this information even if it is almost one-hundred years old.

Over the last twenty-five years I've conducted hundreds of these team building workshops. In the course of the training I ask people to solve some simple basic problem solving puzzles. Most of the people have actually completed them previously. More than 90% of the time people cannot do them. These are intelligent people. They just seem to have lost the ability to think creatively about a problem and tease the solution out of it. But when these same people are put on a team with a minimal amount of coaching their enthusiasm and problem solving skills are rekindled and the results are undeniable.

Even more interesting is the ability of teams to reach *synergistic* solutions. We talk a lot about *synergy* in business. I define synergy as: two or more things working together to accomplish something they couldn't do separately. In normal circumstances, daily team meetings etc., it is difficult to know if any level of synergy has actually been attained.

With the exercises we are able to measure the knowledge of the individual, the team and compare it to expert opinions. On these instruments the lower the score the better the decision. If the team score is lower than all individual scores the team exceeded the knowledge of any individual team member. This means the team achieved *synergy*. The team exceeded the knowledge of each individual team member. The teams comprise of 5-10 people and it is not unusual for them to achieve synergistic decisions.

The team training allows people to learn and practice two important skills required for teams to be effective. They are:

- Interpersonal (people) skills
- Rational (critical thinking) skills

The exercises allow people to practice each of these skills in an interactive way. There are a lot of dynamics in a team discussion. Things can get out of hand and result in very poor team performance. For that reason alone people need a way to practice how to participate in team decision making and problem solving. They must practice how to listen, support and differ with other team members in a constructive way. We found there is just no way in business for people to practice these skills. The exercises fill that gap.

We also found that graphing the performance of the teams is an excellent way to show people how a mental/physical process can produce data. The graph below displays the % of gain achieved by teams on one of these team building and problem solving projects. This training involved 77 teams with 5-8 people per team. Four (4) of the teams regressed and seventy-three of the teams improved their performance vs. the individual results. The average amount of gain by the teams was 60%. Eight (8) of the seventy-seven teams, almost 10%, were able to produce *synergistic* decisions.

When I work with top management they often tell me they've introduced the team concept to their employees so there's no need to train their people. When I ask if they really know how good their teams are at solving problems, they admit they can't.

Basically, management exhorts the employees to work as a team and gives them some problems to work on. Their operational definition of a team is two or more people getting together at a few meetings and talking about a project. As far as knowing if the teams are capable of effective problem solving they don't have a clue. Most of the time they're not even sure why I'm asking about these skills. Managers desperately need to learn more about leading, developing and empowering teams to solve problems and manage all work systems.

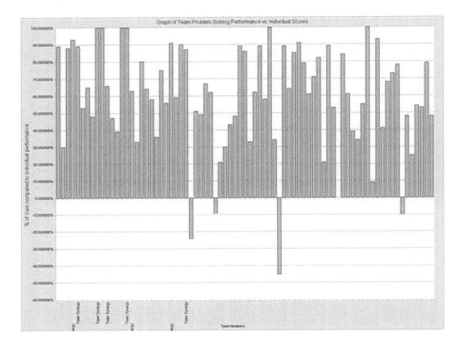

An analysis of how well teams performed

What makes an effective team?

Managers must be able to teach people, what makes an effective team? To do this you first need to define what team means. I think Katzenbach and Smith's definition below is an excellent start:

> *A team is a small number of people with complementary skills who are committed to common purpose, performance goals, and approach for which they hold themselves mutually accountable.* [20]

Along these lines, when I ask people to describe the traits of an effective team they will usually generate a pretty comprehensive and consistent list of characteristics. They are:

- Cooperation
- If a team is to function at all people need to work together.
- Collaboration
- People on teams need to learn how to share their thoughts, ideas and information.

- Communication
- In order for a team to work people need to talk, listen, support and differ about ideas and comments from team members.
- Creativity
- The more ideas you can get about solving a problem the better off you are.
- Have a common goal
- Without a common goal teams struggle and disintegrate.
- Use a structured disciplined approach to solve problems
- This means they start out with a common problem solving method.
- Learn how to reach a consensus to examine, evaluate and rank the alternatives they are suggesting will solve the problem.
- Consensus removes fear from the team process so people can live with and support the team's solutions.
- Be achievement oriented
- The team will apply high standards of excellence.
- On a team each individual can and does make a difference. You do not lose your individual identity just because you are on a team. In our training if an individual can't live with it, he can block the team, which gives each team member a lot of power, authority and responsibility.
- Apply cause and effect thinking but realize they are not closely related in time and space.
- Allow self-set goals – this lets the team set goals management wouldn't even think about.
- Seek feedback from the process to determine what has happened with the team's theories and changes.
- Participation
- Everyone can and should contribute.
- Everyone respects each other.

At some point in our lives all of us have worked on a team. The results can range from sheer joy to being something you never want to experience ever again in your life. But the fact is, teams and teamwork are one of the best ways to get work done and solve problems. When people are given the opportunity to learn how to work as a team and they practice their skills their ability to manage for continual improvement is unlimited.

To understand systems we need people working as teams. Peter Senge argues we must have learning organizations to face the challenges of business. We need to learn how to make cooperative learning in companies the reality of how we manage and solve the problems created in work systems. Some companies are starting to take advantage of teams but no company I know of has realized their full potential.

It's obvious teams and teamwork are going to be an integral part of managing work systems now and in the future. It's also clear we all have a lot to learn and unlearn when it comes to leading and managing them. Teams must be a driving force for solving problems of quality, production and safety.

Organizational problem solving

I think everyone knows there is a difference between solving a problem that only affects you personally vs. a problem that affects two or more people. On a personal level you can attack a problem any way you like. We're all different and each of us has our own way of doing things, including how to solve problems.

But solving problems in an organization presents some unique challenges. You are up against the system and when you push the system, it pushes back. Safety problems are no exception. Safety is subject to the same obstacles and barriers other departments face when it comes to solving problems.

The first order of business for organizational problem solving is to determine if the problems merits the formation of a team to solve it. If the type of problem and its solution is blatantly obvious making the decision is easy. For example, under normal circumstances you don't need a team to change a light bulb. But if you are working on solving something more complex like reducing the number of employee injuries you should start thinking about who you will need on the team.

The team should start by looking at what should be going on vs. what is actually going on. I've seen many teams put a lot of effort into a project and fail miserably because they haven't performed this initial analysis. It looks like this:

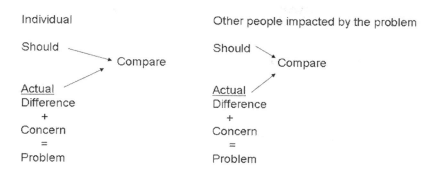

How individuals and organizations solve problems

Suppose you are driving to a meeting along the interstate. It is a clear morning, the road has a smooth even surface, and the weather is great. Your car is in perfect mechanical shape and there are no other cars within five miles of your vehicle. (Obviously this is a hypothetical situation. You're probably somewhere in Nebraska.) You are in great physical condition, 20-20 vision. You just happen to be traveling 10 MPH over the speed limit.

The "should" in this situation is 70 MPH. The actual is 80 MPH. The difference between the should vs. the actual is 10 MPH. Do you have a concern? The answer is probably, no. All of the conditions are such that you're OK.

Now let's add another factor to the situation. Suppose you have a radar detector in your vehicle and it starts beeping furiously. Now do you have a concern? Probably, and the concern is going to grow rapidly. But it's only up to you if you want to take the appropriate action to solve what has now become your problem.

Now take this exercise to your workplace and apply it to what is perceived to be a problem. For example let's say employees have brought up a safety issue among themselves. They are concerned about back pain while performing their jobs.

The "should" = employees should be able to work without any back pain.

The "actual" = employees are complaining about back pain.

The concern = if people continue to do the work as it is now designed they will incur a back injury and require time off work.

A group of employees decides they want to study the problem and come up with a solution everyone can live with to reduce the back pain. They go to the supervisor with their concern and tell him about it. He is under a lot of pressure to make sure parts are delivered by his operators to work stations. He asks if anyone has missed any time due to back pain. The answer is no. He tells the employees he'd like to help them out but he isn't really concerned about it.

In this circumstance forming a team and going through all of the effort to fix this system is a waste of time. The employees should not do it. Their alternative is to let the supervisor know they are disappointed with his lack of concern and they would like to take their data to his superior to plead their case.

I can assure you this is not a rare situation. In the traditional plant the problem would just continue until either someone gets injured or the pressure of production is reduced. Either way, nothing has been done to solve the problem. It also reinforces a passive/defensive culture of avoidance of a problem instead of facing it and solving it. In this scenario, the management infrastructure isn't there to support the team.

If you have a problem and someone involved in it does not share your concern you won't be able to do much about it. This way of managing problems may sound negative but it reveals very quickly those people who have an attitude contrary to continual improvement. It will take an honest effort by everyone in an organization to break down barriers so concerns are addressed and problems solved.

If your company is not into continual improvement you won't get much help in this type of situation. There hasn't been an accident and other numbers will be more important to management. Consequently, overcoming this obstacle will require another skill, commonly referred to as 'beating the system.'

Convergent vs. divergent problems

The British economist B.F Shumacher argues that there are two fundamentally different problems: "convergent problems" and "divergent problems." Convergent problems have "one solution." The more you work on them and study them the more the answers converge to one solution. Divergent problems are just the opposite. They do not have a "correct" solution. The more people with knowledge and intelligence observe and study them, the more they come up with solutions that contradict each other. The problem doesn't seem to be with the individual people but more with the problems themselves.

The fact is divergent problems are a bit more complicated. If you want to travel from your house to your place of work, there may be a correct answer for "What is the fastest way to get from your home to work?" But there may not be any right answer for the question, "What is the best method for making work safe?"

As people work intelligently on divergent problems they can quickly hit a stone wall of ideas. The difficulty is divergent problems just don't have one best solution. This doesn't mean that some ways of handling divergent problems aren't better than others. You just have to keep working on them and use all of your creativity, ingenuity and patience. The danger is to get frustrated and treat the problem as though one solution is the best without digging deeper into things. This is the issue with the concept of root cause thinking for accidents. People start with the viewpoint they are dealing with a convergent problem when in fact most accidents involve divergent problems. When they investigate an accident and find a solution they like they stop there and label it the root cause.

"How to prevent employee accidents?" is a divergent problem although management wants to treat it as a convergent one. Consequently, they spend the least amount of time, energy and brainpower on it. They want a simple direct answer because they want it to be a convergent problem. But behind every complex problem there is a simple easy answer. That is wrong. We must have a more open thought process to solve the divergent problems of safety.

Creative Problem Solving

When you are dealing with a divergent safety problem you will have to think of creative ways to solve it. This means you will have to come up with new ideas and methods. This will be a totally new behavior for most safety managers and workers. Our behavior is constrained not only by assumptions we have of others but also by assumptions the systems and organizations we interact with have about us. Blindly following rules by definition is not creative. Traditional safety management applies four types of assumptions to constrain creative employee behavior[21]:

1. Assumptions safety management makes about us
    (We will not break safety rules)
2. Assumptions we make about safety management
    (The system is unyielding and will not allow any deviation to safety rules)
3. Assumptions the safety management makes about itself
    (The safety system functions correctly, if people would just follow the safety rules they won't get hurt)
4. Assumptions we make about ourselves and others
    (We are powerless to change the safety rules or influence the keepers of the rules)

The problem is, since these assumptions are made to make people conform to the rules they end up stifling any creative or innovative approach to solving safety problems. As a result, when people in management think about safety they think compliance. When it comes to safety, the only creativity applied is to find the most efficient (cheapest) way to comply with the rules.

If managers would only take the time to say, 'OK here's the safety problem, what will it take to solve it?' everyone would be much further ahead. Instead managers focus on satisfying the rule makers, not the people who are directly impacted by safety on-the-job. They often don't know exactly what the safety problem is. Managers should learn to state the safety problem from the point of view of why the individual involved would want to solve it. They should treat the person doing the job as a customer, which requires taking a different point of view. This is very difficult to do for most managers. They will often start with the intention of improving safety for an employee but at the first sign the system is going to push back they revert to thinking of the employee as just some arms and legs or a bionic machine hired to do the job.

We need to do a better job of applying creative problem solving to safety. In creative problem solving you need to look at a problem from many different angles. By taking a different point of view and using different levels of thinking you will begin to use your creative thinking skills. This provides a disciplined strategy of how to define the problem and the solution will come from your ability to think creatively. The approach is quite different than relying only on an "expert" opinion or a regulation for the solution.

The figure below shows how elements of creative problem solving fit together. This approach would help everyone look at accidents from the perspective of systems thinking and develop innovative solutions to safety problems.

Creative problem solving involves looking at a problem from many different perspectives. (Variation) You should look at the order, structure and relations that exist in the situation to see how they work together. (Systems thinking) Determine what level of thinking you are at (Knowledge) and what point of view you are taking (Psychology). Most of the time we forget about the employee's, or more correctly the safety customer's, point of view when trying to solve a safety problem. In doing so the needs of the most important people affected by the problem are ignored.

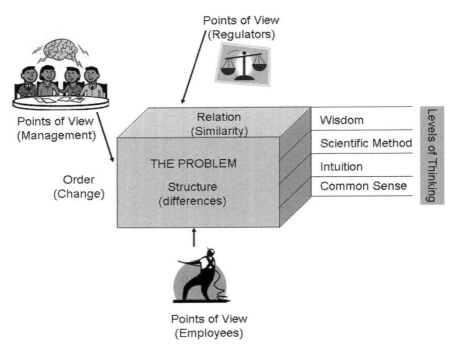

Creative problem solving involves many points of view

The diagram below is an actual example of employees putting their creative talents to work to come up with a creative and innovative solution. Employees were being injured at the work station shown at the top of the diagram. They had a very limited area between the pallets and the box table shown. They were bumping their lower legs against the table sustaining cuts and bruises. The aisle way had a safety line forcing the placement of the pallets close to the workers. A total of 6 employees worked on this operation and the injuries had been going on for years.

The injuries were minor in nature and the workers didn't even report them after the first year. They thought there was nothing they could do about it. The safety department also thought the system was OK since no injuries were documented.

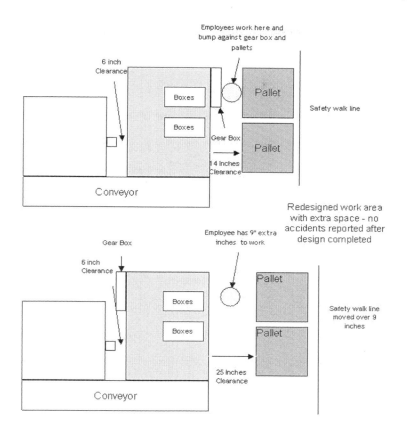

The top drawing shows before and the bottom after the work station was improved

A team was put together after an informal survey in which the workers brought up the situation. They believed if they could get just a little extra space (relation) between the pallets and the table (structure) the operations would be much easier (order) and the injuries would stop. They talked with the safety department to see if the safety line could be moved 9 inches away from the work area. Safety, staffed by a practical person, agreed this would be OK. They also moved the gear box to the other side of the table providing some more space for the workers. Result, the employees ended up with 25 inches of workspace verses the fourteen they had. The job was much easier and safer. No accidents were incurred by anyone after the change. They were having 5-10 incidents per week before the change.

This example shows how all four basic assumptions were broken. First: the employees did not want to break the safety rules but the rules needed to be changed. Second: Employees were convinced the safety manager would not allow them to move the safety line but she did. They thought this rule was cast in stone. Third: The safety department thought the design was functioning just fine. It wasn't. Fourth: This had gone on literally for years. No one thought they could do anything about it so everyone just lived with it.

It also shows how the team used their creativity to work on the structure, order and relation of the problem.

They approached the problem from different points of view, theirs, the safety department and upper management. They changed their level of thinking by collecting some data about the accidents. This gave them some more information taking them to a higher level of understanding. This example shows how creativity can be applied to solve divergent, systemic problems. It's the how all of the methods described should be combined to produce synergistic solutions to common causes of accidents in work systems.

Part 6

Moving forward – leadership for safety

The aim of Part 6 is to examine how leadership needs to be transformed so a company can achieve continual improvement of safety. Transforming an organization requires leadership at all levels.

"We have industrial modeled organizations running postindustrial businesses." Stan Davis, Future Perfect.

"The new leader is one who commits people into action, who converts followers into leaders, and who may convert leaders into agents of change"

"Managers are people who do things right. Leaders are people who do the right thing." Warren Bennis

The question is, if you believe there is a better way of managing safety, how do you do get your organization to use it? You must remember you are going to be stepping on some toes by telling people the things they've been doing are no longer correct. (After having a discussion about what I do for a living with a friend of mine he exclaimed, 'Tom, you're not a consultant, you are an insultant.') But history has numerous examples of ideas people thought were true until someone came along and proved them wrong. In the sixteenth century Copernicus proved the model of the universe written about by Ptolemy and followed for over fourteen hundred years was wrong. Copernicus was able to confirm the facts with new mathematics and a new theory. The earth went around the sun and his way of thinking proved it. There was no way of bringing back the old truth.

That doesn't mean people readily accept a new idea willingly. As Thomas Kuhn pointed out in his essay The Structure of Scientific

Revolutions, scientists have been known to deny or even ignore new evidence that refutes their paradigm.

In his fourth edition of Psychology in Industrial Organizations, 1973, Norman R.F. Maier explains how to improve productivity by reducing time and effort reaching for tools:

> *For example, if a large number of bolts are to be used to fasten two pieces of metal together, the naïve procedure is to drill each hole and secure each bolt separately, thus completing all the operations with one bolt before going on to the next. The more efficient method would be to mark all drill holes; then drill all the holes; next put on the bolts and fasten the nuts by hand; and, finally tighten all the nuts with a tool. Reducing the number of times the tools are changed is one of the simplest and commonest methods of eliminating wasted motions.* [22]

I point this out because I find it interesting that Maier, who had a PhD. in psychology and obviously an intelligent person, pronounces the batch-and-queue method superior to the single flow approach. For some reason most people have a tendency to believe working with batches is the best method to perform repetitive work. (Many, if not most American managers still naturally choose the batch and cue method vs. flow. Even if they say they would choose a flow method when they set up an operation they still organize it as a batch and cue process.) This thinking is in direct contrast with the ideas of flow, advocated by Henry Ford. He reduced the amount of effort required to assemble a Model T Ford by 90 per cent back in 1913. He did so by switching to continuous flow in final assembly which is the opposite of the batch-and-queue system described by Maier in 1973.

Starting in the 1950's Taiichi Ohno and Shiego Shingo advanced Ford's ideas at Toyota and achieved continuous flow in small lot production. They learned how to change tools quickly and right size machines so process steps could be done next to each other. Ohno's approach to operating the shop floor is counterintuitive to batch-and-queue methods. But it has proven to be a superior method when it comes to efficiency and cost. It's a new manufacturing paradigm and even highly intelligent people such as Dr. Maier couldn't see it. (Then again, Japanese read from left to right so maybe they are able to truly look at a system differently than we do.)

The Toyota Production System is considered by many to be one of the best examples of lean manufacturing. They have not been secretive about how they set up their operations. American managers have studied it and visited their plants. GM even works in a joint venture with Toyota called NUMMI with the intention of learning the system. Nonetheless, American manufacturers have great difficulty when it comes to mastering lean manufacturing. They've made some progress but just can't seem to make the complete transformation.

I see the same lack of progress in safety management. The traditional Taylor/Heinrich paradigm prevents people from seeing and practicing a new ways of managing safety. First they want to see how someone else does it before they will try it. And even if someone else is doing it they still don't like to change what they are comfortable with. (I think that is why people like to benchmark so much.) Joel Barker calls this "paradigm paralysis." He points out however, when the paradigm shift occurs, everything goes back to zero. No matter what your position in the old paradigm, first in the market, leader in technology, best reputation, subject matter guru, you will be starting from scratch in the new one.

Mr. Don Milroy, a former VP of Masco Corp, and one of the most insightful, people oriented managers I know, gave me a good explanation for why American managers don't change. He said it's revealed in the equation:

$$R = E$$
Reason equals **E**xcuse.

A manager's explanation for not doing something includes all kinds of reasons that justify their inaction. Basically these are just excuses for not trying something new. Inexplicably, when it comes to safety, managers like to use "the system" as an excuse to cling to the status quo. They have paradigm paralysis. They can't escape from the old safety rules they know and are familiar with.

Years ago I made a presentation to a local safety council on the topic of applying continual improvement theory to safety. A safety manager in the audience made the comment he wasn't going to "drink that kool aid." He was referring of course to the blind obedience and subsequent mass suicide of the followers of Jim Jones. He admitted some of the things I presented made sense but he just wasn't willing to accept the basic philosophy.

As I've been saying throughout this book, the goal of the traditional safety paradigm is to meet safety specifications, which means doing so is "good enough." But people don't realize if this is your main objective, your results will vary as much as possible. It's because once you've meet your specifications you don't need to worry about any variation between them. No more work needs to be done. Deming's concept of variation is to have consistency, to be on target with minimum variation from the target. To do this you must work continually on the system so the outcomes vary as little as possible from the target and then work to create harmony between all parts of the system so it can accomplish the aim of the system.

Comparing how managers work with the two approaches shows how different the theories really are. Take safety training. Suppose there is a legal safety training requirement for employees. A traditional safety manager would have all the employees attend a safety training class and verify it was completed by making everyone sign in. Once the class is over the employees can go back to work. He may even have them take a test and set a minimum level of competence. He's done his job. The company has "met the specifications."

Buy no one knows how much the employees really learned from the training or how long they will retain it. How could they? Some people may understand only 50% or 70% and others over 90% of the information. Yet all of them are OK to go to work. The safety training would be deemed "good enough." But in reality all kinds of variation has just been introduced into the system and management bears no consequences for ignoring it. Only the workers will pay the consequences in the form of injuries due to lack of understanding and using the information.

A manager committed to continual improvement would approach the training differently. She would start off requiring everyone to learn 100% of the information. The employees who score less will have to repeat the training until they can score 100%. (She lives the credo, if the students haven't learned it's because the teacher has not taught.) She would work to remove the variation so at the very least, everyone would have the same information about safety before they could go to work.

When they return to work she would follow up with them to determine how well they have retained the information and applied it on the job. She would create a feedback loop so people could come to her for answers to questions they might have about the training and how to apply it. She would also find out what needs the employees have about training. How can it be made to be more effective? More enjoyable? More user friendly?

In a culture of continual improvement, when it comes to worker's safety, settling for the status quo is never good enough and there are always problems. We must manage safety so we can find problems and then solve them. No excuses.

Quality and excellence in safety management

Ultimately, changing how you manage safety is about the quality of safety in your company. What does the word quality mean when applied to safety? If you were to examine what traditional safety managers actually do you would have to conclude they believe quality of safety is about complying with safety specifications and/or acquiring some sort of certification.

Companies spend a lot of time and money on safety seeking some type of recognition such as the VPP designation by OSHA or to be ISO certified. Personally, I fail to see how seeking recognition by others has anything to do with improving oneself. I find it interesting that the automotive companies, including Toyota, have experienced some of their highest quality recalls rates in recent history. This is in spite of the fact most of their suppliers are ISO certified and praise has been reaped on them by other consumer watchdog agencies. I think a high quality safety effort can only be achieved when people are given the theory, tools, methods and authority to fix safety problems that invariably exist in any system *before* they cause an accident. When safety management achieves this it is operating at its highest level of quality.

There's plenty of evidence to show traditional command and control cannot be reconciled with continual renewal and improvement methods of safety management. Quality of safety in a command and control management system equates to achieving compliance. This is the same as continually improving obsolete products or service. No one will purchase obsolete excellence. Quality of safety in a continual improvement management system should always be about making safety better for the workers who are the true customers of safety management.

A few years ago I was working with what is considered a world class company when it involved customers and quality. We were talking about using the theory of continual improvement for safety when one worker stated,

"When we have one defective part reported, management pulls everyone together and brings it to our attention. If we have two defects, all hell breaks loose and a team is set up to do a complete investigation of what went wrong in the system to make sure it doesn't happen again. But if an employee gets injured the supervisor immediately sends the person off to the first aid station. His next move is to make certain someone can replace them as soon as possible to keep the line running smoothly."

Actions speak louder than words and in this case the message to the workers was the quality of our parts is more important than the safety of our people. Unfortunately, this scenario takes place in various degrees everyday in the U.S. It's not because the supervisor doesn't care about his workers. It's because in this culture when it comes to safety it's not as important for him to solve safety problems as it is to keep production going. It's the old persecution of production again.

We have to make a transformation away from accepting patches and workarounds as the acceptable method for solving safety problems by managers. One way to change this approach is to develop problem solvers – lots of them at all levels. Helping people learn, practice and apply problem solving techniques should be how a safety person spends a large amount of their time. Then give them the opportunity to apply these skills on-the-job.

Where are you starting from?

A person using his cell phone calls a friend and asks for directions to the airport? His friend responds, where are you at? I can't tell you how to get to the airport unless I know your location first.

Some people see things as they are and ask why. I see things as they could be and ask, why not? George Bernard Shaw

Implementing a new safety paradigm means you are going to ask people to start thinking about safety in an entirely new way. How you convey this message will depend on your level in your organization and the level of the people you are working with.

Everyone has a circle of influence. The position you hold may determine how much influence you can exert. If you are top management you can have a much different impact than an hourly person who just started working for the company. But, no matter what position you hold your effort can and will make a difference if you handle yourself properly.

Your influence depends on just how the company is set up and how you relate to the people you interact with. I've met some hourly employees who have a very large circle of influence and some managers who have a very small one. The circles start small and entail things you can change yourself then they extend outward to include things you can change through the help of others and all the way out to areas that no one has control to change.

Helping people see a new way of managing safety is going to be very, very difficult. Some of the challenges will seem insurmountable so you will need to be thick-skinned and have a sense of humor. You will be able to change some things on your own and some will require a lot of help by others. You must learn how to handle paradoxes. You will need a sense of urgency and be patient at the same time. You powers of persuasion and ability to make a compelling argument will be tested daily. The bottom line is, as you are going to have to learn how to beat the system,

Everyone knows change is difficult to achieve no matter what position you hold in an organization. Top managers say the most difficult thing for them to do is to change things. Guess what, the lowest level employees say the same thing.

Machiavelli talks about the challenge of changing a system as early as the 16th century when he said:

> *"It must be remembered that there is nothing more difficult to plan, more doubtful of success, nor more dangerous to manage then the creation of a new system. For the initiator has the enmity of all who would profit by the*

preservation of the old institution and merely lukewarm defenders in those who would gain by the new."

The subject of change is beyond the scope of this book. People have spent their whole life studying change and how to make it happen. The things I want to reiterate about change are:

1. It's difficult
2. You can and must plan for it
3. It never happens exactly as you want it to
4. It's necessary for continual improvement
5. It's going to happen whether you are involved or not so you may as well get involved

So let's take a look at things you will have to consider when you are trying to change how safety is managed in your organization.

Success starts and ends with culture

"I came to see during my time at IBM that culture wasn't just one aspect of the game, it is the game." Louis V. Gerstner Jr., former chairman, IBM

"The board should establish a budget for changing the culture over a period of five or ten years so that top management can devote its efforts to building KAIZEN along with its normal duty of realizing a profit." From "Kaizen, The Key to Japan's Competitive Success" by Masaaki Imai

Kelleher and Barrett believe culture is one of the most precious things a company has, so you must work harder at it than anything else. From the book, Nuts-Southwest Airlines' Crazy Recipe For Business and Personal Success

Culture in a company is obviously a big deal. An in depth discussion about culture also goes way beyond the scope of this book but everyone can use some basic principles about culture when working on the transformation. Just trying to define it and understand what it means is a challenge. Basically culture can be defined as:

Shared values (what is important) and beliefs (how things work) that interact with an organization's structures and control system to produce behavioral norms (the way we do things around here).

Culture is one of those things that exists and has a huge impact on your business but something you will never be able to see. It's the glue that holds an organization together or can tear it apart. The cultures at Enron and World Com are examples of cultures gone awry. In his book, The Toyota Way, Jeffery Liker states, *"The purpose of this book is to explain the Toyota culture and principles it is based on."* He describes how Toyota creates a positive constructive culture for change.

I once heard culture described as the broth in soup. You can add the best ingredients, the finest carrots, onions, potatoes, etc. but if the broth of the soup is lousy you're going to have lousy soup. If you have a lousy culture, you are probably going to have a lousy company. Management programs such as TQM, Six Sigma, Lean, Balanced Scorecards, will not work when coupled with a lousy culture. And there have been plenty of failures of these programs in a lot of companies over the last twenty years.

If a system is the product of the interactions of its essential parts, culture is the product of interactions between its people. That means a company may have an overarching culture but it also has many sub-cultures. Most people believe culture is a mysterious element of organizations and it can't be measured but this isn't so. There are a number of good diagnostic tools that exist to measure culture and your company should take advantage of them. If you do your homework and use an effective diagnostic tool you can get a good handle on what type of culture exists in your organization. In most instances, everyone, especially management, is in for some real surprises when the results of these surveys are reported. It's a matter of determining what type of culture exists in your company, what do you want it to be and how will you make it happen? When examining culture, companies must be prepared to work on change.

> *"NASA's initial briefings to the board on its safety program espoused a risk-adverse philosophy that empowered any employees to stop an operation at the mere glimmer of a problem. Unfortunately, NASA's views of its safety culture in those briefings did not reflect realty."* [23]

This is just another poignant but tragic example that when it comes to culture companies say one thing and do another. There is no denying that culture has a direct impact on safety. The effects can come in many different ways. If a company has a culture in which short term thinking is the norm managers will shortcut safety in the name of doing what they believe is the right way to manage. They cut costs and don't worry about things they can't see. Unfortunately, as I have been arguing throughout this book, the causes of most accidents in any operation are the things you can't see. These include but aren't limited to the consequences of choices made to please demands to achieve short term profit.

Safety professionals have jumped on the culture bandwagon along with everyone else and now talk about having a "safety culture." I'm not sure what that means but it sounds good. Peter R. Scholtes says, "If it means anything, culture should describe the day-to-day experience of the ordinary worker."[24] If the quote from NASA above is any type of indicator it is apparent you can't separate safety from the overarching culture of an organization. It is just too easy to publish a safety statement and not back it up or protect it from the culture that drives the company. (That is why the 14 Points are modeled after continual improvement methods.)

If a manager gets his operations through one day without an accident, even though the way safety is managed is terrible (Which is very possible since people will do everything they can not to get injured.), he will assume safety is fine and operate in the same fashion the next day. In his mind he believes he is a doing a good job of managing safety. He is keeping safety costs low and there haven't been any accidents. But absence of a negative doesn't mean you have a positive. When the time comes to spend time or money on safety he won't do it willingly and there will be no incentive to make him do it, until it is too late and someone gets seriously injured.

The answer is to have your company refer to the 14 Points often and use them to guide decisions about safety. If you do this you will create a positive constructive culture modeled after continual improvement. The organization will be one in which the ordinary worker can and will be able to contribute to improving safety every day. The 14 Points will guide the behaviors and actions of everyone so they will do the right thing when it comes to making decisions that affect safety of the systems in the organization.

Leading the paradigm shift

"If you're a "normal" person, you tend to believe any studies that support your current views and ignore everything else." Scott Adams

"Criticism has few terrors for a man who has great purpose." Benjamin Disraeli

"He didn't give us the answers. He just showed us how to get there." Bill Walton, describing John Wooden's coaching techniques at UCLA

How do you start and sustain a paradigm shift in an organization? Well, I'm sorry to disappoint you but I don't have the answer. And as far as I can see, no one else does either. It truly is a divergent problem. Not that transformations haven't taken place and been successful, they have. One of the best narratives about making a total transformation was done in his book "A Better Idea" by Don Peterson. Peterson led the transformation of Ford Motor Company in the 1980's and it lasted into the 90's. Then Ford lost it under a series of failed regimes. Ford is now doing another transformation under the leadership of Alan Mulally. In the last ten years Motorola and Boeing always seem to be working on some sort of a comeback that entails a new paradigm of management.

I do know that asking people to change how they manage is equivalent to asking them to change their religion. Taylorism or Neo-Taylorism is so ingrained in American managers they just can't think of any other way to manage and they will resist change at almost every turn. Adding to the problem is we are still defining the new management model for the 21st century. I also know that a successful transformation requires someone stepping up and being a leader.

One reason managers cite for not changing is they would like to get started but the timing isn't right. (R = E again.) They don't think their organization is ready for this approach. This raises the obvious question, if not now, when? But waiting for the "right time" to get started in the methods of continual improvement to manage safety is nonsense. People's health and physical well-being is at stake every day so the right time to start improving safety is right now. Nonetheless, most safety managers prefer the status quo. You can't blame them. They've been living in the status quo world so long they don't know anything else. These people are not comfortable leading change. You will meet a lot of these managers.

So here is the dirty little secret everybody knows; there is no easy way of making continual improvement of safety performance a reality in your business. I wish there was a magic remedy or instant pudding but I haven't found it yet. When I do I'll be the first one to publish that book.

There are just too many variables involved. Some things such as your thinking style and your ability to lead, you can control. Most of them you cannot. These include the culture and subcultures in your company, your immediate boss's thinking style, your level of authority, the performance of you company for business and safety, etc. Negative aspects of any one of these could stop the transformation process dead in its tracks. If more than one negative exists, as is usually the case, it can make the task daunting and seemingly impossible. Not understanding how to work with and manage these barriers results in safety managers stuck in a no-go mode. But one word of advice, don't let R = E get in your way.

There are many excellent definitions of leadership. Basically a leader is someone who people will follow to a place they wouldn't go on their own. A leader must be willing to help and serve other people. To be a leader you have to believe totally in what you are doing. You will be asking people to step outside the boundaries of their current safety paradigm to work on the insoluble problems of the current one. The bottom line is, this takes guts because the new paradigm doesn't provide all the answers either. It just opens the door to finding new ones. Leaders make maintaining the status quo more dangerous than trying something new.

You must keep one goal in mind at all times. You are on a mission to lead a new safety management model in which employees aren't just passive participants or treated like bionic machines. They are real people who want to contribute to the success of the company and all of them have intrinsic motivation to do a great job without being injured. Great companies know employees deserve to be able to do their jobs safely every working day. No one is asking for a better way of managing safety so you will be challenged about every change you introduce. The barriers to making the transformation are real and they will not be easily removed but if you don't do it, who will?

The futurist, Joel Baker, says you manage within paradigms and lead between them. You cannot expect top management to take the lead initially. The last time I checked there were no courses on safety management in any of the MBA programs out there. All top managers say that safety is their number one concern. What else can they say? With very few exceptions this is not the reality ordinary workers experience everyday. Top managers usually work from one crisis to another so unless safety is causing them a problem they are going to pass that daily responsibility on to other managers. There are no examples of CRISP out there for top management to emulate because the theory is so new. The companies that do have good safety records have mastered the Neo-Taylorism/Heinrich approach and will see no reason to change. They are confident the old adage, if it ain't broke, don't fix it, applies to them.

I believe the situation in safety parallels what happened in quality in the 1970's. Back then American companies had most of the markets cornered so their level of quality was improving but not at the rate of the Japanese companies that were just starting to sell in the U.S. So, American managers were stuck in a state of denial about what needed to be done when they began to lose market share to their new competitors. A lot of these companies never recognized what was going and they never recovered. Safety management cannot afford to do this. The quality of safety management must be improved.

When it comes to change it helps to have an example to show people what you are trying to accomplish. Some have used benchmarking for this. But there will be very limited examples of companies that have truly used continual improvement theory and practices for safety. More than likely you will have to build them by yourself in your company. You will be able to use examples of quality management and relate how these can be used for safety. In his book, A Better Idea, Donald E. Peterson, former CEO of Ford offers 29 case studies of improvement projects.

If you are a safety manager or supervisor you should start on your own project with the goal of accomplishing something couched in terms top management will support. Of course in safety there are always the altruistic reasons and safety can always be related to costs, delivery, quality and morale. (Who among you is against safety?)

Over the years I seen three major reasons transformation fails:

1. Being new to this, as everyone is, you are going to make some mistakes. The one committed most often is choosing the wrong project to start out with. The most frequent mistake is taking on a project that is just too big, i.e. reducing the number of back strains in an entire plant. These types of projects, sometimes referred to "boil the ocean" or "cosmic"

issues, are just too challenging for people to tackle when they are just learning what this whole approach is all about.

2. Having limited knowledge about your subject. You will underestimate how much there is to learn and unlearn. You are going to find the Taylor/Heinrich paradigm is embedded in manager's DNA. So much so, they don't even know it's there. To counter all of the reasons and arguments for not changing you will have to be prepared with examples and knowledge to win people over. Changing religion and management is not easy. It will take every ounce of leadership and knowledge you possess and more. This doesn't mean you must be a wise and old to get started. It means you must keep learning no matter how much you think you know about continual improvement now.

3. When you push the system, it will push back, sometimes with a vengeance. I've been in many conversations with safety and operations managers who possess what is called "articulate incompetence." They can make a very convincing case for why the traditional safety management model should not be tampered with. Your patience and powers of persuasion will be tested to the max. You will have to counter their objections with a compelling reason to try a new approach and this will not be enough. Safety, like religion, is a very emotional subject. You will have to win people over in a very inoffensive way. If you can't build your case with positive persuasion, the system will destroy what you create.

In other words, you must be prepared to handle plenty of criticism, failures and setbacks. Remember, good judgment comes from bad experience. Use each attempt as a learning opportunity. Keep track of what went right and wrong and share it with the people who are working with you. I can say from experience you will have to be ready to become a leader, not just a cheerleader. That means you will be placing a target on yourself and everyone else not committed to your success will probably be taking shots at it.

You have to practice what you preach and that means using the vocabulary and ideas of continual improvement. Don't just learn the words; learn how to carry the tune. You must be in this for the long haul and since you are going to be messing with the paradigm or the rules of safety it will take courage. If you are new to implementing change you are in for some big surprises, not the least of which is how people cling to the old ways of doing things and shoot down any new ideas or concepts.

You should start by finding out how the company applies its quality programs/processes. There is a direct parallel between quality and safety and you should leverage this at every opportunity. i.e. defects and accidents are the same in the sense they are created primarily by the system, not by individuals. Seek out people, especially managers in position of power, who may be open to this new approach. Then make friends with them by discussing how and what they can do to help you. If you try to help them you will lose control of how the projects will be done and you can't afford that. Don't be afraid to ask a favor of someone with power.

A basic approach

I have introduced Continual Renewal and Improvement of System/safety Performance (CRISP) to a host of managers and hourly employees for the last twenty years. It starts with training a small number of people on how to apply the Plan, Do, Study and Act cycle to examine and improve safety in your systems. This learning process can be applied to every aspect of what you do to design and improve safety. It is identical to the typical problem solving protocol in all learning organizations. These people are also trained on team building exercises described in the section on teams and safety management. They also learn the basic theory of continual improvement and how it works for safety management.

Once they have been trained they select a project that will not exceed their ability but not so simple it is a "no brainer." This is not the time for "stretch goals." Basically there are three types of projects; No-brainers, low-hanging fruit and cosmic problems. Classifying them can be as much of an art as a science. The goal is to have teams work on low hanging fruit issues. The issues should not be too challenging but large enough so the team will get an opportunity to apply what they've learned to solve them.

The teams should then literally go to work out on the shop floor. They will experience what it is like to collect data and create flow charts of processes. They spend time interviewing other employees and get the Voice of the Safety Customers into the projects. They develop operational definitions and brainstorm solutions to problems. They should determine if their project is dealing with common or special causes and learn how to react to them appropriately. They will learn how to fix the system.

All of this is documented to build a data base of lessons learned and problems solved. I've talked with too many managers in companies large and small who tell me how knowledge walks out the door when people retire or leave the company. Or people explain they have solved a particular problem years before, but all the information has been thrown out.

Whenever possible, at the end of each of project have the safety team present back to the highest level of management so they can see what the people have learned. The teams should be mostly people from the line who have applied the tools and methods of PDSA. The results are always impressive. Usually to the point where management sees how they should take advantage of the brainpower of everyone when it comes to safety.

Basically, the strategy is to have people continually apply the PDSA cycle to build a learning organization. Applying the PDSA becomes "the way we do things around here." Of course this sounds simple but as with any deployment activity, it is terribly hard. Problem solving on teams is a skill to be learned and improved over time with practice. There are always some people who learn faster than others but everyone can learn something new on each new team project. All the teams will experience some sort of failure. Fortunately the PDSA cycle allows for this because the changes advocated by the teams are always implemented on a small scale to test a theory and see how it works. If the change produces a positive result you can expand it. If it doesn't work, you can put things back the way they were and try it again and again until you do see an improvement.

In all the years I have been working with people in this workshop the teams have never disappointed me. They all come together in a unified, positive approach to solve the problem they select. No team has ever completed their project on the first day. They all end up working on their projects for weeks before they finish it or close it out. Some companies are obviously more successful at keeping the teams going than others. There is unanimous agreement that CRISP is a better way to manage safety than command and control.

Plan, Do, Study Act Cycle for safety

PDSA—Action Steps

I. Plan: Develop a Plan to Improve Safety Performance

Step 1: Identify the opportunity for safety improvement. Work on a chronic safety problem – low-hanging fruit. Use data. (Feedback from workers and their self-set safety goals, pareto analysis, hazards reported, accident rates, run charts, SPC charts, etc.) Focus in on what is possible. Find out who cares?

Step 2: Document the present process. What is the actual? (Number of hazards, accidents, first aid cases, flow chart the process, identify problem areas, cause and effect.)

Step 3: Create a vision of the improved process. What should it look like? (SCAMPER report, Do another flow chart, brainstorm, affinity, force field analysis.)

Step 4: Define the scope of the improvement effort. Who? does What? by When? (Action plan, control plan)

II. Do: Carry out the Plan:

Step 5: Pilot the proposed changes on a small scale, with safety customers, over time.
(Action plan, deployment plan)

III. Study: Study the Results

Step 6: Observe what you learned about the improvement of the process. (Data analysis, run chart, SPC chart, Pareto Chart, Feedback from customers)

IV. Act: Adjust the Process, based on new knowledge.

Step 7: Operationalize the new mix of resources. (Expand the change to other parts of operation as required)

Step 8: Repeat the Steps (Cycle) on the next opportunity.

Beating the system—how to operationalize the 14 Points

Over the last twenty five years I have been told by almost every single safety manager I've met that they can't apply continual improvement to safety until they get all of their traditional safety duties completed. It's their excuse for not doing something that will require them to put forth extra effort to learn something new and do things differently.

Problems in a company, especially safety problems, are too big and too pervasive to be attacked in a sequential fashion. That means you can't wait to complete one before you start work on another. Like first we'll attack quality and when that's done we'll attack safety and when that's done we'll attack relationship problems with our employees and after that we'll work on culture. In reality you may have to work on all of them at the same time. This sounds counterintuitive but it's the way the world works. It means management must be ready to trust people and in most instances they will respond in kind.

People start out with companies wanting to come to work and do a good job. They don't come into your company as "deadwood." If they do you've got a bad hiring process. In today's economy good management involves creating an environment where people are brought into a work system and provided guidance and insight of how to succeed. They learn how to go about doing things to contribute and improve quality, productivity and safety. And in most cases they will be asked to do so without a manager looking over their shoulder every minute of the day. If you're not hiring deadwood make certain your culture isn't creating it.

Without making it sound too simple here are some actions to help you introduce the 14 points to your organization.

Learn to work with people to obtain their cooperation and commitment to be part of the transformation to build a shared vision of just what safety will look like in your company.

Meg Wheatley has a wonderful theory about change. She believes the world only changes when a few individuals step forward not when top-level programs or ambitious plans are put forth. It starts with everyday people having a conversation about things they care about and then taking action. I can't think of too many things more important than being safe on the job for people that work for a living. It is fairly easy to start a conversation about safety with people at work. I've done it many times.

How many times in your life have you heard the phrase, "A little competition won't hurt anybody?" Unfortunately, this philosophy, which is deep-seated in the Taylor/Heinrich approach to managing people and one of the most wrong-headed ideas applied to continual improvement, is a major obstacle to applying the 14 points and improving safety. When it comes to facing a challenge, solving a problem or improving something, cooperation and collaboration are always more effective then setting up internal competition where inevitably someone in the organization is going to lose. You will not get anywhere in any organization unless you cooperate with others and they do the same with you. Why would you want to make someone lose and then have them as a partner? Who wants a partner that is a loser? Why would you want to make someone feel as though they are a loser?

Study how the executives think about safety. Examine any safety policy and determine how you can show management that a new way of managing it will help improve safety performance. Do this in terms the level of management you are dealing with will understand. Juran speaks of a "Pyramid of Power." People speak in different ways at different levels of the pyramid. People at the bottom tend to speak in terms of things. People at the top tend to talk about dollars and profit. Safety can be made to appeal to all levels of the company. Always try to use the correct language for the audience you are talking to. The fact is every CEO does care about safety but they face even more pressure to care more about profit. Safety is all about reducing the worst form of scrap, employee injuries. Always have the ability to relate what poor safety performance does to the bottom line when talking with upper management.

If a manager believes competition is a good thing in either small or large doses, as most American managers do, he is going to have a difficult time understanding that cooperation and collaboration are the building blocks to a better world. CRISP enhances and enables high productivity with an emphasis on cooperation between internal departments and people. You should use every opportunity to keep this idea in people's minds but make sure you do it in very subtle ways. You will make very little progress in gaining acceptance of this idea if you try to force it on a person who worships at the altar of competition. Meg Wheatley's advice is rock solid. A pleasant conversation where listening is involved will do more to help people understand things than any power point presentation.

An important step to building a shared vision will be to find out what does safety mean to your company. Ask things like, "When it comes to safety what do we stand for? What are we trying to do?" Points 1 and 2 are the principles you will use for creating a constructive culture for safety. Continual improvement has to replace command and control. You must strive to make safety a top priority for your managers, right up there with quality. Not just in words but in deeds. If you are a member of upper management put people's safety ahead of products and profit on your list of company values. It will be the hardest value to live up to but it will win the hearts and minds of everyone. Improving safety always leads to better performance in all areas of any company. This includes production, quality and profitability!

You will have to demonstrate the new way of thinking about safety to everyone. You will have to encourage people to look at the world of work through the lens of profound knowledge and the 14 Points. This will help them gain a better, deeper understanding of why accidents happen and how to react to them when they do. You can do this whether you are the CEO or an hourly employee. Make continual improvement of safety a way of life at work and home.

Broaden your concept of safety to include the customer focus. Everyone has to understand the most important customers of safety are the workers, not management or outside regulators. (You aren't going to ignore the regulators but you are going to focus exclusively on them either.) If you take care of worker's safety they will become better suppliers to the company and to your customers.

Make sure people know and understand the reasons you are going to change your safety management system. The transformation is not about doing what you did in the past only doing it better. It is a new way to approach safety at work with new theories, methods and actions. A big change will be to push decision-making and authority down to operations. This does not relieve management of its responsibility to lead safety and remove barriers that prevent people from working safely at all times. This will take a leap of faith for many managers but that is exactly what is being done at companies who truly understand the principles of lean. The responsibility of the person doing the actual work is evolving to where they take on the role of managing and doing. They are simultaneously a knowledge and a production worker.

No matter what your present performance is or has been in the past, it can be improved. Even if you don't have any obvious safety problems (which is unlikely), absence of a negative doesn't mean you have a positive. Empowering the workforce to fix safety problems in the system is absolutely critical for being proactive.

Whether you know it or not, your work systems are changing every day. Systems seldom perform the way you plan over time. Processes change, people come and go, new products and services are created. All of this creates variation. Employees know more about the problems of safety in production and service than anyone else. They must be able to respond to situations quickly. Management cannot fix and improve the system without the active participation of the workers. The purpose of an excellent safety effort is to have employees who are engaged, enthused and empowered so they can study and improve everything about safety everyday.

You must have an operational definition of what empowered means. You can empower all the people some of the time and some of the people all the time. But you can't empower all the people all of the time. What will the new level of authority be when it comes to making safety improvements? Will teams be able to resolve their safety customer complaints? Will they be able to allocate funds to fix safety problems? How much? How often? Specific details should be created so everyone knows where they stand. To start, teams should have pre-approved authority (within limits) to spend money to correct problems. Of course, they should always look for ways to save money, not spend it. Not too surprisingly, over the years I've found employees working on teams do a much better job of watching how money is spent then managers.

Do everything you can to change the thinking of senior and middle management about safety.

Although you believe safety should be managed using the same theory and philosophy of continual improvement that doesn't mean the CEO and other managers will see things that way. There are no large scale examples of the new way to manage safety. There are no benchmarks out there so they won't know or appreciate what you are talking about. You will be building your own version of CRISP to produce excellence for safety.

The biggest obstacle for mangers when it comes to change is to let go and/or get out of the way. (This harks back to Lee Iacocca's advice for managers, lead, follow or get out of the way.) When it comes to safety, without realizing it, managers have been trained not to trust employees. This model just won't work in today's economy. It is outmoded and inefficient. Management must work to build trust between employees and understand they will work with management to improve safety. Conversely, employees must give managers a chance to start over so the new approach can work.

You will have to seek out colleagues in the company who are interested about learning a new approach to safety. Meet with them on an informal and regular basis. You will have to introduce them to the new concept of serving safety customers, the employees, so the system can meet their needs. This will probably make them very uncomfortable. When it comes to safety they have been trained to control everything, especially the workers who report to them.

For many managers waiting until the "time is right" to do something is part of their management DNA. I have a long list of managers I've dealt with over the years who are still waiting for the right time to "get started." As I said earlier, if not now, when? For these managers the right time usually never arrives. This is not acceptable in safety. While you are waiting, people can and do get hurt. Learn how to use a force field analysis to address these types of situations. Don Peterson, who led one of the biggest business turnarounds at Ford in the 1980's said you can't wait for one stage to be completed before you start another. The process like life comes at you fast and furious. You will have a lot of things going on at the same time. Cultural change is always like that.

It will be important for people to become systems thinkers. When it comes to safety, the system is most of the problem. The problem is you can't see most of the things in the system that cause accidents. People must learn how to think about the system and what effect it has on the safety of workers. Non-systems thinkers are incapable of doing this and will always focus on the people when things go wrong, especially an accident. It's the easiest way to identify a non-systems thinker.

You will have to help people understand and use systems thinking for safety. This will stop them from faulty conclusions about what causes accidents. They will realize the difference between symptoms and causes. They will also think about things you can't see like the interactions and interdependencies that create most of the accidents, and what must be done to fix the system to make it right. They will stop accepting frivolous solutions to serious problems.

Peter Scholtes said people don't mind change. They just don't like being changed. This essence of this book is to show there are better options when it comes to managing safety. We need to educate ourselves so we have choices. Where is it written you must manage safety the way it was done in the past? There is always a better way, you just have to work a little harder to discover it.

We need to move away from the American mindset that safety standards that are cast in stone. Some standards are not the best way to do something and should be updated when necessary. Traditional safety managers seek best practices as a cure all. This will not work.

Do not wait for the complete participation of top management in everything you do. It will not happen. They are too busy doing many other important things. It's true the company won't get the full benefit of the 14 Points and profound knowledge without the backing of the CEO, but you can do a lot of improvements and use them to convince the CEO and others this new approach is the right way to manage.

Determine what are managers willing and capable of doing for teams.

What kinds of decisions are the middle managers willing to give up? What will they support? Most mangers don't want to give up any power. This is why it is so important for managers to make a concerted effort to understand what teams can and cannot do. Be careful to make this transformation slowly yet consistently. Since our history is steeped in Taylor's and Heinrich's theories, employees aren't familiar nor are they comfortable with the team approach. Even today, with all of the positive things we know about teams, managers and employees aren't that experienced in leading, managing and working on teams.

Most people didn't sign up for the increased responsibility required to make the transformation. It takes time for people to learn teamwork, develop problem solving skills and use their new power to solve problems. It has been observed that employees don't really like the decisions other people make for them but when given the opportunity they have difficulty making those decisions by themselves. Teams will have to learn how to use the PDSA cycle so they can make good decisions on their own. Managers will also have to learn to trust the choices teams make. Although this approach will do more to control the system than any method used in the command and control world created by Taylor and Heinrich, I've seen managers reject it almost immediately. They do so because it takes away the power they have worked so hard to obtain. But in the world of continual improvement this line of thinking is irrational and irresponsible.

When appropriate establish teams as the driving force to fix the system.

Although we are still learning how the new management model will look in the 21st century it is apparent teams will play an important role. The synergy that is created when people do work together is just too important to deny or ignore. We must break down barriers created by command and control on the shop floor and replace them with teamwork. The great difficulty in making things better is the misunderstanding of the whole system created by hierarchy. When teams are organized to manage processes, the real needs and Voice of the Customer can be addressed. There is no doubt about it, improvements are accomplished faster and better when teams are used to study and improve the system.

Some people believe once they have been on a team and undergone some team training they know how to manage teams. They are in for a rude awakening. Team management is just one element of the new management system. Teams will integrate with all other facets of getting work done faster, easier and with better quality. When teams manage "things" such as budgets, strategy and day-to-day work activities, then you will be able to say your company understands and uses teams properly. We are just scratching the surface of how people work in teams and do it effectively. We will have to discard everything we "know" about managing to make teams work for safety. If your teams are still overseen by a manager or a supervisor that second guesses them, your company is applying the superficial approach to teams.

Teams are not used for everything. Organizations will have to learn when teams are appropriate and when they are not. (Teams should work on common causes is one thing you should learn first.) This is no small feat. Very few people have the ability and experience to do it. But it is where we must go and safety should take the lead. Most companies have some form of team management and most of them have a very long way to go when it comes to doing it well

Share data, learn how to turn data into information and turn information into knowledge.

Companies never have enough money or resources to solve all of their problems. You will have to prioritize what problems you will address first. You must learn to work on the trends and patterns of the system. Employees understand this and will cooperate with management to utilize resources wisely. When people understand "why" they are doing something they will take care of the "what" and "how" it has to be done.

Use the data you have about safety so the system will talk to you. We often fail to use safety data intelligently – if at all. To do this we will have to apply statistical thinking. The data you collect can be analyzed and turned into information. Once you have information you can analyze it further, make predictions and test your theories. This will create knowledge about how to improve safety. Working in this manner we can work to change the system to impact the common causes that create accidents in the first place. This leads to better productivity.

Don't worry about the problem employees but don't ignore them either.

The first question often posed by mangers when starting the transformation is "What do we do with the troublemakers, the accident prone employees?" (My question is always, what are we going to do with the managers who will put forth the biggest resistance to the new approach?) When Dr. Deming was asked, what do you do with employees who are considered deadwood? He responded, did you hire it, or did you kill it? It's easy but futile to stay focused on the trouble makers. The fact is these people usually didn't start out that way. The question to answer is, did the management hire the people with bad attitudes, which would indicate a poor management practice, or did the system create it? Either way it's still up to management to fix the system. It's the only way to turn attitudes around and it has been shown to work. There are some people, managers and hourly, who just won't work out. If you do have them, it is best you part ways if they truly aren't going to try.

In recent years there has been a move to recognize the very worst behaviour of employees. Scott Adams was one of the first to call for companies to "eliminate the assholes." He even made it the number one activity for his conceptual model of a perfect company. [25] More recently, Robert Sutton has written and entire book titled *The No Asshole Rule: Building a Civilized Workplace and Surviving One That Isn't*. The problem has become so perverse even our academics have been forced to finally deal with it. The simple fact is, mean-spirited people, managers or hourly, who don't take other people's feelings into consideration are not worthwhile keeping around. They do too much damage to morale and have probably caused quite a few employee accidents along the way. I have no data on this but in this case common sense is more than adequate to figure it out.

Generally employees who do best on teams are people who enjoy other people and seek pride and joy from work. Frederic Herzberg's research in the 1960's and verified many times since, showed excessive rules and company policies are the major contributor to de-motivating employees. [26] After years of working in a system that destroys intrinsic motivation, it will take time to bring people around. But in fact many people will respond immediately if they are asked to contribute and help fix the system. They can do this when working on a team. As these employees work on the new process others will join in on their own volition and at their own pace.

Of course you would like to see everyone on the bandwagon from the start but this just isn't going to happen. You can't fix past mistakes with proclamations about a new program. People will view it as a new flavour-of-the month. People must *see* evidence of the new way on the job before they will believe it is real. Vaughn Beals past CEO of Harley

Davidson when it started its transformation said, "It may take longer than you want but once it starts it will have its own momentum."

Sustain a learning organization.

Employees don't often get the opportunity to learn about new theories and how they can be applied. Knowledge is needed to move any safety system forward. Training on job skills is fine and necessary to do a job. But people need to build knowledge about how a system works. To have knowledge requires you make a prediction to test your knowledge. People need to learn how to learn and solve problems so they can study and understand how to improve any system.

Don't expect employees to impart their new found knowledge immediately. Unlike training for a job skill, which can take employees to a high level of performance very quickly, knowledge is learned and applied over time. It is always given up voluntarily. We are all inelegant learners and there will be plenty to learn. People will have to learn how to work on a team and how teams can work together and share knowledge. There is no time frame for this. It starts and it continues. It never truly ends.

In today's economy the company that uses a structured, disciplined approach to gaining knowledge and has a central depository for it that is accessible is the one that will create jobs and profit in the short and long term. That is what a true knowledge management system is all about. There was a lot of hype about knowledge management in the 1990's but it has not been successful to this point. Not because it isn't a good idea we just haven't been able to apply the discipline to any degree. Leaders in business will eventually learn how do it.

Learn how to make safety systems operate on target with minimum variation from the target.

It is easy to set goals. It's done all the time. However, setting a goal (quality or safety) isn't the same as aiming your system to hit the target. Everything that you do with employees is part of the aim of your safety system. (Common causes) How people are treated everyday when they do their jobs (culture) affects outcomes (scrap, rework, accidents). Setting goals is easy. Adjusting your aim is the hard part. What's important is, what method will you use to achieve your goals? Will you be a leader or a manager? Teams need both to be successful.

Just meeting safety specifications will not suffice in the new economics. It allows excess variation to exist or ignores it. A better goal is to have all parts of your system working together so they can hit targets with minimum variation. This is a goal, a purpose everyone can relate to. Variation and how to control it is a key to managing systems effectively. But just operating on target still isn't enough. It will take leadership to have people believe that this is the way we do things around here.

For the most part, American managers cannot tell you what each process in the system will produce. Nor do they care to find out. If they are asked to explain why the variation in a system exists they will blame it on the carelessness of workers, their sloppy work habits, saboteurs, poor attitudes and behaviours or all of the above. The fact that variation can and should be measured is foreign to them and they don't have a clue as to what to do about it if they did measure it. There are many components in any work system. The basic ones for safety management are; people, materials, methods, machinery, equipment, environment and culture. Each one is part of the whole. They are all interrelated, interdependent, interrelated and interactive. If they don't work together the system cannot achieve its goal.

Your performance depends on how the elements of your system function together. You must aim properly to make the system hit its targets. Improve your aim and you will improve your system in degrees previously never achievable. You must work upstream to improve the aim of a system. Everyone should strive to keep each part of your system working cooperatively with the other parts.

Stop de-motivating people

We are reminded daily about how important it is to motivate people. Unfortunately, a lot of what we are told about motivation simply isn't true. Most is more folklore than fact. One idea, accepted without question, is that extrinsic motivation is one of the best ways to get workers to perform better or work harder. The more we learn about what happens when we employ extrinsic motivation the more surprises we uncover.

For instance, we've known for years that pay is not the great motivator many believe. Survey after survey tells us employees do not rate pay as the number one satisfier at work. Of course people want to be paid well for work. On a superficial level it seems that if you pay more you can get more from the workers. Again, research, evidence and reality paint quite a different picture. If you doubled employees pay could they double the quality or quantity of their output? Could they cut accidents by 90% over both short and long term? They could not. As I've said before, beating horses can only make them run faster for a while. You end up having people pre-occupied about things that really don't matter and not paying attention to things that do.

And yet everyday in the U.S. companies employ safety incentive programs as a management tool for safety. Instead of setting up a system of internal competition to motivate people we need to strive for internal cooperation and collaboration to achieve goals. Without it you will never achieve synergistic performance that will truly solve system problems. There is more than enough competition outside your organization you can't control. Why make things worse by bringing it inside too?

When a supervisor has been warned not to have any scrap, waste, rework or accidents in their operations he is probably being asked to control something about the system which is surely beyond his individual ability. (If we've learned anything it's that no one person controls a system.) He is often held accountable for these system problems in his personal performance appraisal. Internal competition heats up and the real causes of system problems are never addressed. Instead he looks for ways to make the numbers look good in the eyes of his boss. People have been known to bury the numbers or cook the books in these types of situations.

There is an enormous amount of research that contradicts our imbedded belief that rewards are the best way to motivate people. The fact is rewards do work but only if you want people to work for rewards. If you want people to do a quality job, search for ways to let every employee contribute to improving the system. Most importantly create a culture that does not destroy the intrinsic motivation everyone has to do a good job and be safe while doing it. Work on finding and removing the de-motivators at work. If you are having problems with the idea of not worrying so much about motivating workers I recommend you read or re-read the landmark HBR article by Frederick Herzberg, "One More Time: How do you motivate employees? And Alfie Kohn's outstanding work, "Punished by Rewards."

The question we must ask is, if motivating people through rewards is not the answer for improving quality and productivity what good can come of using it for safety? Using the incentives to make people behave safely becomes a farce as a safety management method.

Have patience and always remember, this is not going to be easy.

Rome wasn't built in a day. The command and control model advocated by Taylor and Heinrich will not be dismantled in a day either. But the sooner it is the better off everyone will be. Keep moving forward, like a tortoise everyday. Remember you are in this for the long haul. All systems are broken and can be improved. This is especially true of safety in any work system. When you start to push the system it will push back. Persistence, patience, humility and perseverance are absolute necessities if you are to prevail.

The traditional approach to safety has managers accept the system as it is and try to get the most out of it. In contrast, safety managers who have learned profound knowledge and the 14 points are constantly looking for ways to improve the system. They know blaming employees for not complying with the rules is not a good option.

As a result, they work to create trust between management and employees. Employees learn their jobs involve more than just showing up and collecting a paycheck. In addition to normal production responsibilities, their role will include studying safety of the system and helping management solve problems within that system.

Managing safety using continual improvement requires a new level of thinking in which employees are viewed as safety problem solvers, not the reason accidents occur. Management must continue evolving to meet customer demands. Layers of middle management, created to monitor and control employees, are not needed in new management models and will probably never return. Even if supervisors could motivate workers and there is little evidence around to show they could, the fact is they won't be around in the new management system.

Employees will have to be self-motivated to do their jobs well and to do them safely.

But the safety system has to be managed by someone. The new safety management model gives this responsibility to those who do the work. The people who help gather and analyze data and make decisions that directly impact safety performance. They are the new knowledge workers.

Although continual improvement is revolutionary for safety management, it is an evolutionary process. One of my clients drew a timeline to show they would move from the traditional command and control safety methods to continual improvement. Ultimately they would phase out their dependency on Taylorism and replace it with an approach more aligned with CRISP.

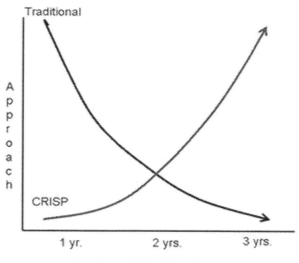

Time line of transformation

A day in the life of a traditional safety manager

For a moment let's consider a hypothetical company and look at how its safety program is run by Joe, a safety manager trained in conventional safety management methods taught in colleges and used in most organizations today, even well established high quality, lean companies. Joe has learned and truly believes his job is to run an efficient, effective safety department. To do this, he sets up activities to monitor and control employees and supervisors behaviors and strives to ensure compliance with company safety rules and regulations.

Much of his time and anyone who works in his department is spent providing government-mandated safety training and conducting company safety inspections and audits. He negotiates next year's safety goals with top management and various department heads. He sets safety standards for employees and tracks their performance, conducts accident investigations and recommends corrective action to prevent future incidents. He believes a manager's job is to hold people accountable for their individual actions. If an employee questions a safety rule he reminds them it is their obligation to abide by them. They are made to protect them and he can't change them. Deep down inside, Joe believes the majority of accidents are caused by unsafe actions of workers. Consequently he is seeks ways to motivate them to do their jobs with no injuries. Joe considers himself a hard working manager, a person of high integrity.

As his job gets more demanding, Joe adds staff or uses outside consultants to help complete safety training, safety inspections, accident investigations and data collection. He recruits other managers and some hourly employees to serve on the safety committee, which establishes goals via management by objectives. He teaches this process to supervisors, and a mutually agreed upon goal for accident reduction is set (typically between 5 and 10 per cent). These goals are included in the supervisor's performance appraisals.

Joe implements a sophisticated program to collect accident data. Each department is monitored and compared, and changes in monthly rates must be explained to corporate management. Since managers are held accountable for accidents; they in turn hold their employees accountable. Departments are ranked in the order of who has the most accidents and which ones have made the largest improvement (reduction of employee accidents) in safety performance. He pits one department against the other to foster what he refers to as friendly or healthy competition to keep their interest in safety at a high level.

Joe's idea of working upstream is changing employee behavior. To ensure that he is motivating employees to work safely, he establishes safety incentive programs, which reward employees or departments that achieve pre-set safety goals. Typically, the goals are zero accidents for a certain length of time. If goals are reached, gifts or monetary rewards are presented at a banquet. If goals are not met, no awards are given, and the program is restarted or replaced. Joe is constantly reminding people to use positive reinforcement to motivate people to work safe.

Joe believes a good safety manager is one who establishes an efficient, effective safety management system. His main responsibilities are:

- Monitoring managers and employees to ensure they follow his directives correctly
- Setting the safety goals for employees, departments and the company as a whole
- Rating managers, department and divisions for their ability to follow safety rules and instructions
- Evaluating employees to see whether they demonstrate safe behaviors
- Holding people accountable for their actions or safety violations
- Re-educating workers after an accident and returning them to work as soon as possible. If an employee has multiple accidents, Joe informs management, and that employee is reassigned or replaced if necessary.
- Providing numbers to show improvement. He explains poor results by identifying those who are ruining the program: this identifies the truly poor performers.
- Conducting safety audits and reporting results to top management and local management.
- Interacting with safety regulators to ensure safety violations are kept at a minimum.

In short, Joe has created a top down, command and control bureaucracy to monitor and control things. His ultimate goal is to meet all safety specifications. He is a single event thinker and focuses on how to control employee's actions. Top management appreciates Joe's approach. They like it and see no need to change it.

Safety management with profound knowledge

Contrast Joe's approach with that of Shannon, a safety manager who has learned to look at work through the lens of profound knowledge and is guided by the 14 Points. She knows her job is to facilitate a constant effort – safety does not start and stop depending on the most recent performance. Shannon understands that as a manager, she works *on* the system and the employees work *in* it. To improve safety performance, she understands she will need their cooperation, knowledge, input and ideas of how to improve safety standards and get the voice of the employees in the safety system.

So Shannon strives to provide leadership; helping everyone – top management, middle management and employees – learn why the company must improve its safety performance every day. To manage safety she decides to use continual improvement methods to study and fix the system. She has abandoned the traditional approach of safety which is to ensure compliance with safety specifications.

Over the years she's learned that having an overriding goal of meeting safety specifications actually guarantees the goal will not be reached. She guides her daily work routines by reminding herself and other managers about the 14 points. She doesn't cite them verbatim but verbalizes them in a way that makes sense to the people she is interacting with. She does keep them posted prominently on her office wall.

Employees see Shannon as a manager who is exciting to work with and they describe her as having passion for safety. They share her passion and want to help make it happen. They think of Shannon as a leader, not a boss.

Shannon has evolved into a systems thinker. She focuses on underlying causal factors linked together which result in accidents. She has disciplined herself to always step back and look at the whole situation. She works on critical behaviors of management not workers, realizing that manager's control the processes that can create error inducing systems or operations filled with hazards that lead to most employee injuries. Especially when it comes to budgeting for safety.

Rather than replace employees, she strives to change the management-controlled safety system so employees can help improve it and perform their jobs without fear of injury or reprimands. She knows it takes years for people to become good problem solvers and she is patient with them. She works hard to ensure employees will have no fear of reporting safety problems to management. Because of her diligence top management has fully implemented a policy that an employee can stop the line if they believe a serious safety issues exists. She encourages all employees to join safety improvement teams.

Because of her profound knowledge she looks at safety differently. She believes employees are her customers. They benefit from her leadership and her ability to remove barriers that prevent them from being able to work and improve safety every day.

She constantly tries to find ways to get the voice of employees when it comes to safety into the work processes. She knows this is required to improve safety and productivity. She understands employees know best where safety improvements should be made. They face the problems of variation every day that challenge safety performance. Production is filled with variation that impacts the safety of everyone.

Shannon engages people in casual conversation to keep change at the forefront of safety. She has seen people take charge after simple, direct and open conversation that starts with one simple idea. They end up working together to make a difference. She often asks workers, what do they think is possible and who cares about doing it?

She studies modern manufacturing methods that require standardized work but sees the paradox that you can't standardize people. She understands that in some ways people are all the same but they come in all sizes, shapes, mental capacities, ages and have different backgrounds. That's just part of the system. Every day people bring a boatload of variation to the job. She has seen diversity of all kinds become the strength of a team. She can't and doesn't want to make everyone the same.

She strives to leverage their skills and knowledge so she asks for their help in designing and improving the work systems to accommodate them and all of their variation. This human variation must be reconciled with standardized work. This requires employees to study the system everyday and gain knowledge so they can predict what will happen to people when they do their work. She teaches them how to be good problem solvers and apply these skills to safety issues in their work areas.

To Shannon, accidents are worse than producing scrap. When an accident occurs, a person's physical and mental health is reduced. And the damage doesn't stop there. She understands accidents cause employees to lose respect for management. She knows safety is an outcome of the system. She understands events that cause accidents occur randomly, that variation exists in everything and this common cause variation is the primary reason for accidents. Each job is different; also each employee is unique, making it impossible to design a job for the "average" worker. The average worker doesn't exist. Half of the people are above and half are below average. For Shannon, being below average just means you are on the other side of the line. And people cross the line in each direction every day.

To enable management and employees to work together, Shannon teaches them to apply systems thinking to safety management. She knows management and hourly people have difficulty communicating so she teaches them how to use the common language of statistics. She stresses cooperation between workers and management. Instead of a mechanistic view of accident causation, they look at accidents as a system outcome. She has set up a library of books and videos about quality and the employees are encouraged to use it to learn more about systems thinking and customer focus. She sprinkles her conversations with employees with terms used in lean manufacturing and quality methods. She relates these concepts and terms to safety.

She uses statistical process control charts to provide a new way of looking at accident rates. She helps all managers and employees learn the philosophy of statistical process control so they can chart their safety performance and understand what it means. The charts show whether accidents are out of control due to special causes or are affected only by common cause random variation. The charts also help supervisors stop blaming employees for accidents and focus efforts on system problems. They no longer tamper with the system. They fix it.

If the charts do show a special cause people work together to identify it and determine if any action should be taken. Everyone is always encouraged to suggest ways to reduce the number of accidents. But she doesn't use a suggestion box. She has face-to-face contact and listens to them in person. Then she helps them take action on their ideas. She listens to employees and responds to their needs.

Shannon establishes teams who help identify, rank and solve production safety problems. These teams do not merely make suggestions about safety improvements, they apply the Plan, Do, Study and Act" cycle for safety:

- They use problem-solving tools such as process flow charts, pareto charts and cause and effect diagrams to develop and implement system changes.
- They study these changes and evaluate their effectiveness. As a result of their changes they ask, did safety get better? Worse? Stay the same?
- If the changes don't work, the team sticks with the problem and makes improvements until its causes are eliminated and the system is improved. Problems don't solve themselves.
- They apply the PDSA cycle in a disciplined way so they can be creative in their solutions.
- They work on being innovative and creative when looking for solutions to problems.

Shannon's has learned her most important activity is to remove barriers that prevent employees from doing their jobs safely or improving the system. That means they get time for training on problem solving and team participation. She has worked hard to show management this training pays off in reduced costs and higher productivity and employee morale. She does not try to change employee behavior through extrinsic motivators, but relies on intrinsic motivators such as pride in their work, the joy of achieving flow at work and self-preservation to keep safety foremost in their minds. She knows employees must own the safety program for it to be successful.

For her, working upstream involves making sure she is considered an important member of the management team. She has learned how to beat the system of bureaucracy. She is involved in strategic decisions watching out for new methods and processes being proposed by managers. She has learned how to relate safety to production costs and has convinced management that safety pays. She wants to make sure safety is always considered in the design stage of production so hazards are addressed proactively when it is more cost efficient and effective. She knows her presence drives a positive safety culture in the company. She has trained employees to do the same. She also knows that once production is running safety can be improved but to do this takes discipline on everyone's part. Her safety teams are always looking for low-hanging fruit or the basic safety problems. That's because once you have solved a problem, the system is always subject to variation and like dust on your living room table tops, new minor problems return regularly.

She knows extrinsic motivators destroy intrinsic motivators, so she does not use safety incentive programs. She believes her time and budget is better spent making certain real accident causes (poor management systems) are changed and eliminated. She does encourage celebrations and helps employees set them up. Celebrations are not contingent on meeting a specific goal. They are done to nourish the efforts of people to make safety better. Occasionally even a failure is celebrated because she knows people worked hard on it and learned something from the experience.

After working with Shannon, employees view a safety goal of 5 to 10 per cent reduction as "nonsense." As customers, they want 100 per cent reduction of injuries. Because they have learned systems thinking they understand how challenging this goal is and want to work with management to reach the goal. They know they must help management by participating on teams since systems are too complex to be understood by just one person working alone. The teams learn how to beat the system and change it for the better.

Shannon does not think of employees as human capital. She treats them as equals, people who just happen to have different job responsibilities. She sees them as thinkers and creative human beings who want to contribute to work. She values, solicits and respects their opinions and ideas. Therefore, she does not name a "safe employee of the month award" or display "motivational" safety posters. If employees want posters they create their own and do more than that – by themselves. They measure their safety performance and use safety teams to make continual improvements on their own ideas. Employees set their own safety goals and work to meet them using the new approach to manage the system Shannon has taught them. Because of Shannon's leadership employees know safety is a joint responsibility between management and employees. Shannon often reminds management of their responsibility to lead the safety effort by example every day. She often tells people, "If you want employees to be safe on the job, give them a safe job to do."

She convinces supervisors time spent on safety adds value to the company. Not only does it improve safety, it impacts morale, productivity and quality. She teaches management how to respond to safety problems in the same way it does to production problems. Employees are trained on problem solving techniques and given time to apply the PDSA cycle to fix the system. They are not afraid to notify management if a safety issue comes up on the line. They face them head on and have the authority to fix them. For Shannon, safety is serious business but it is a very enjoyable work activity. Safety and production is always a win-win situation.

Using the new approach to safety management people like Shannon will help companies travel down a new road where they will achieve a level of safety performance once thought impossible. The important questions are: Which road will you take? When will you start?

Thomas A. Smith is President of Mocal, Inc. He and his wife Shelley live in Lake Orion, Mi. He can be contacted at 248-391-1818. His e-mail is tsmith@mocalinc.com or at www.mocalinc.com.

Suggested Reading Material:

2020 Vision, Davis, Stan M. and Davidson, Bill
A Better Idea, Peterson, Donald E.
A Study of the Toyota Production System, Shigeo Shingo
American Samurai, Lareau, Peter
Cracking Creativity, Michalko, Michael
Dr. Deming Management at Work, Walton, Mary
Dr. Deming's Profound Changes, Delvaigne, Kenneth and Robertson, J. Daniel
Four Days with. Dr. Deming—strategy for modern management methods, Latzko, William J. and Saunders, David M.
Future Perfect, Davis, Stan M.
How's All This Work Going to Get Done?, Blohowiak, Don
If We Only Knew What We Know, O'Dell, Carla and Grayson, Jr., C. Jackson
Innovation and Entrepreneurship, Drucker, Peter
Hard Facts, Dangerous Half-Truths & Total Nonsense, Pfeffer, Jeffery and Sutton, Robert I.
Jaming—The Art and Discipline of Business Creativty, Kao, John
Kaizen – Imai, Masaaki
Kan Ban- Just-In-Time at Toyota, Productivity Press
Leadership and the New Science, Wheatley, Margaret J.
Lean Thinking. Womak, James P. and Jones, Daniel T.
Management Challenges for the 21st Century, Drucker, Peter
Managing Without Management, Koch, Richard and Godden, Ian
No Contest, The Case against Competition, Kohn, Alfie
Normal Accidents—Living with high risk technologies, Perrow, Charles
Nuts! Southwest Airlines Crazy Recipe for Business and Personal Success, Freibert, Kevin and Jackie
Out of the Crisis, Deming, W Edwards
Post Capitalist Society, Drucker, Peter
Principled Center Leadership. Covey, Stephan
Punished by Rewards—The Trouble with Gold Stars, Incentive Plans, A's, Praise and other Bribes, Kohn, Alfie

Quality or Else, Dobyns, Lloyd and Crawford-Mason, Clare
Quality, Productivity and Competitive Position, Deming, W. Edwards
Sacred Cows make the Best Burgers, Kriegel, Robert and Brandt, David
Teams, Tools and Technology, Mankin, Cohen
The Change Masters, Kanter, Rosebeth Moss
The Deming Management Method, Walton, Mary
The Deming Vision, SPC/TQM for Administrators, Fellers, Gary
The Dilbert Principle, Adams, Scott
The Fifth Discipline, Senge, Peter
The Five Pillars of TQM, Creech, William
The Leaders Handbook. Scholtes, Peter R.
The Machine that Changed the World, Womak, James
The New Economics, Deming, W. Edwards
The New Manufacturing Challenge, Suzaki, Kiyoshi
The New Shop Floor Management, Suzaki, Kiyoshi
The Quality Secret, Conway, Bill
The Six Sigma Way, Pande, Peter S., Neuman, Robert P., Cavanagh, Roland R.
The Story of Psychology, Hunt, Morton
The Wisdom of Teams, Katzenback, Jon R. and Smith, Douglas
The No Asshole Rule: Building a Civilized Workplace and Surviving One That Isn't, *Sutton*, Robert New York: Warner Business Books, 2007.
Thinking About Quality, Dobyns, Lloyd and Crawford-Mason, Clare
Today and Tomorrow, Ford, Henry
Toyota Production System Taiichi Ohno -, Productivity Press
Turning to one another – simple conversations to restore hope to the future, Wheatley, Margaret J.
Understanding Statistical Process Control. Wheeler and Chambers
Who Moved My Cheese?, Johnson, Spencer M.D
Why Things Go Wrong, Fellers, Gary
Workplace 2000, Boyett, Joseph and Conn, Henry
World Class Manufacturing, Schonberger, Richard J.
Zen and the Art of Motorcycle Maintenance, Pirsig, Robert M.

End Notes

1. Barker, Joel Arthur, *Future Edge*, William Morrow and Co., 1992, p. 166
2. CRISP is the registered trademark of Mocal, Inc.
3. FW Taylor, "Principles of Scientific Management", 1911. p. 16.
4. Dobyns L., Crawford-Mason Clare, *Quality or Else*, Houghton Mifflin, 1991p. 101
5. Delavange, Kenneth T., Robertson, J. Daniel, *Dr. Deming's Profound Changes*, Prentice Hall, 1994, p.24-37.
6. Heinrich, Herbert W., *Industrial Accident Prevention*, McGraw Hill,1950
7. Perrow, Charles, *Normal Accidents, Living with High Risk Technologies*, Basic Books, 1984, p. 23
8. Deming, W. Edwards, *Out of the Crisis,* MIT Center for Advance Research Study, 1986, p. 314
9. Sandburg, Jared, *Wall Street Journal*, Cubicle Culture, page B 1, Dec. 13, 2005
10. Delavigne, Kenneth and Robertson, J. Daniel, Chapter 2
11. Dobyns, L. and Crawford-Mason, p. 30
12. Deming, W. Edwards, *The New Economics,* , MIT, 1994, p. 92-95
13. Ackoff, Russell, *Beating the System,* Berrett-Kohler, 20054, p. 16
14. Savary, Louis M., Crawford-Mason, Clare, *The Nun and the Bureaucrat*, CC-M Productions Inc., p. 50.
15. Senge, Peter M., *The Fifth Discipline*, Doubleday, 1990, p. 68-69
16. S.I. Hayakawa, *Language in Thought and Action*, Harcourt, Brace & World, 1964, p. 297
17. Deming, W. Edwards, *Quality, Productivity and Competitive Position*, MIT Press, 1982
18. Tribus, Myron, *The Germ Theory of Management*, American Quality and Productivity Institute
19. Scholtes, Peter, *The Leaders Handbook* 1998, McGraw Hill, p. 353
20. Katzenbach, Jon R & Smith, Douglas, *The Wisdom of Teams*, Harper Business 1993, p 45.

21   Ackoff, Russell and Rovin, Sheldon, *Beating The System*, Berrett-Koehler Publishers 2005, P. 28.

22   Maier, Norman R.F., *Psychology in Industrial Organizations*, Houghton-Miflin 1973, p. 272.

23   *Columbia Accident Investigation Report* issued by NASA, Chapter 7, August 2003.

24   Scholtes, Peter R., p. 178

25   Adams, Scott, *The Dilbert Principle*, Harper Business, 1996, p. 321.

26   Herzberg. Frederick, *One more time; How do you motivate employees?* Harvard Business Review, February 1968